RADIANT DROPLETS OF GRACE FROM THE ABOVE

BIRENDRA KUMAR SHRIVASTAVA

RIGI PUBLICATION

RADIANT DROPLETS OF GRACE FROM THE ABOVE

By

BIRENDRA KUMAR SHRIVASTAVA

Originally Published in India

ISBN: 978-93-95773-62-1

Printer: RIGI PRINTERS
Published by RIGI PUBLICATION

777, Street no.9, Krishna Nagar
Khanna-141401 (Punjab), India
Website: www.rigipublication.com
Email: info@rigipublication.com
Phone: +91-9357710014, +91-9465468291

PREFACE

"Radiant droplets of grace from the above"

As the title of book indicates Aspiration received from time to time have there own specific purpose only to aware the Sadhak (Aspirant) with total directives of Shri Maa and Shri Aurobindo and there dream vision.

Whole universe of cosmic Rhythm is Associated with deferent prayers of Shri Maa to bring done the Real Heaven to the Earth by evolution and transformation through Integral Yoga of Shri Aurobindo by Applying intuitive knowledge hence things may by seen "As it is".

what the Mother conceived since birth by inner consciousness decided by HER Agenda is the total surrender of each soul till the objective of new ERA is obtained is seen in shuttle physic by the grace of the Lord, provided each person is ready by his desire and confirm by the readiness in Real sense As only mother knows.

Then devotees or person either with knowledge, intelligence if they want to study – 'these aspirations' with quietened mind they may know and understand the different ideas meditation equations by subjective consciousness.

further they will aware by their Instinct and Distinct knowledge. only Grace of Mother Entrust the Soul purpose of each Sadhak that how Superman is Sworn through the sunlit path and Supramental world is working in full Swing only Supreme knows through Bhagwat Muhurt.

then Ascent and descent, offering and Surrender in Each soul in each moment by psychic being takes place will serve the purpose of objective of this written- Document.

As per aspiration received since year 2007 to year 2021, Date wise and time wise compiled with different Diaries and formed this Book.

Finally, we should pray to Mother:

<u>"Prayer"</u>

O divine Mother,
By Utilization your
Light and Energy
To the whole
Universal consciousness,
Let this Earth
Transform and
Breath in a
New Convention- Yug
ever
Charged by Divinity
Always we are
Great full to you.

Further You have to pretend Theory and invention of integral Yoga- within your Heart and Soul, what Mother Further needs for your birth and births.

However An spiritual Sphinx-Life Awaiting you welcome **It** with quite awaken and Awareness.

GRATITUDE

Here I am obliged to my Guruji **Shri A.P. Khare ji** Resident of Panna (M.P.) Shri Aurobindo Follower, further extended his great Support of inspirations to me as title of the Book he Suggested and help to Bring this English Book to the Devotees of Integral Yoga of Shri Aurobindo in the Wide Platform, Further **Shri A.P. Khare** who confine his devotion to Shri Maa and Shri Aurobindo Since last 60 years, delivered his Talks throughout India in different Shri Aurobindo Societies, centres by brilliant knowledge. His captive intuition knowledge insisted me always He Suggested and supported and guided me in different field of Spiritual knowledge.

I am also Grate full to professor **Shri Suresh Pratap Singh** posted at Amarpatan District Satna (M.P.). An inventor of inner collaboration of Spiritual different Studies and Vedica Excellent knowledge. He always Guided me in the Field of Spiritual knowledge of this Book.

I put my obligation to **Dr. Suman Cocher** at Shri Aurobindo Society Indore (M.P.) and **Shri Manoj Sharma** chairman Shri Aurobindo Society M.P. State Committee I am also Grate full to **Dr. R.B. Shrivastava** (My uncle) Shri Aurobindo Society Branch NOWGONG M.P. for his Guidance and Support me always.

I am thank full to the Panter's Group of Auroville Specific to **Sahana Uppar ji** for design of front cover of this Book.

I am grate full to my typist **Miss. Manisha Khatoon** for typing all my documents and helped in Editing of this Book with Hard labour and concentration.

this Book title **"Rpadiant Droplets of Grace from Above"** is offered to the Lotus Feet of Mother.

RADIANT DROPLETS OF GRACE FROM THE ABOVE

CONTENTS

03-06-2007 mor 06:00 a.m.

SHAVITRI

Regrading "Shavitri"- it should be represented by configuration of different Minds, Wisdom, knowledge and different planes with Audo visual range so as to simplify for different followers of this mission, it may be different colors, sound, speeds, moods graphs, and Para Psychological drifting every chapter volume, canto -should be very-very simplified by means of their grifting and research disciples which is required a new door to be opened for such type of brilliant knowledge we should spread up all over world.

03-06-2007 night. 07:00 a.m.

METHODOLOGY

Indian Methodology You have changed mentioned in the Ancient provokers what is required then?

Choose what caretaker appraised in your personal and Impersonal activation Dynamic consistency in chronological reference may be dealt accordingly.

10-06-2007 morn. 06:30 a.m.

NEW WORLD

Peace, lives in prominent layers, and every layer has it's own quality there are some enable, sincerities come from unknown but desired in heart tackle the different moods in relaxation.

The only foundation on which all the Burning Topics, have their on replies when questioned either in dark or light cross your present limit of different thoughts imagination go to the source where----- **New World** awaits -aspirations and their fulfillment objects converting every work without attachment of any type of passion and Wisdom and Knowledge come from Ego, thence the main Aim, enlighten in the vision of "your self" which is the main object.

15-06-2007 morn. 02:15 p.m.

SHRI AUROBINDO

He started the project work till the different births, completed (with cognition).

Remove the mask of illusion and dust of different Ideologies which create fiction and confusion. Adopt one principal- Idea and philosophy of Discoverer of promised transformation of Earth. To change the enthusiasm of occult, mobilization of thoughts in different planes to give them the inner console direction.

To give creative mountain to meditation through the better source of supreme, to come out from psychosomatic and unconscious inabilities in the light of awaken spark abilities and bring this world in a one platform who only breaths in freedom from different sorrows. Ego's Conspiracies, Mind, Wisdom, brain- driven desires and mensuration where all the Human personalities work Awake and sleep in the shine costume of super mind and supramental convectional Authorities.

27-06-2007 morn. 06:30 a.m.

SADHNA

Miracle never bricks the condolence. Desirous mind always seeks disposition. Knowledge further believes, un end manutention have clear paths to gain target but the showering power contributes limitation with Body, and Brain.

Intuition forwards those in the light of grasping habitats self produced energy charged time to time with spirits of salvage potentiality spheres come from Eternal Sources of Grace.

There are different circles of golden indemnities empowered have different approaches but the Heart has to inaccrochable exercise multiple difficulties to awake it's (credible) incredible conscious which contributes immortal role, represents, superficial gleam, It's that connectivity which interlink all the omnipotent and omnipresent faculties Internal and outer orbits of soul and Body, finally to adjoin the main object of supramental adjacent inabilities.

07-07-2007 morn. 07:00 a.m.

SUPRAMENTAL COMMITMENT

This world is significance of the matter converging continuously same is diverging every body, live, a live, plant, Flowers, Leaves, Trees, Animals, living jeans at Earth sky water – interacting and needs peace and prosperity- investing properties --- attracting the love everywhere through the God only he immense the Light to- talk listen See, Walk, means all types of work through Body and inner sense, so feel him everywhere, what show he is also vast decor- what He desires that is desire of every body but in true sense of great understanding come through soul only.

HE is not thinking like you that is why your way and Aim is different, but if you think like him by going deep intention of his governing power of Internal soul: so both of you will be in the same condition then only you may understand not only but work like him in all the sense so truth and beauty which is the ultimate Aim to divert and convert your body and soul appropriate thinking of super Humanity of great lovers of soul like Shri Aurobindo and brimmed Hearted Shri Maa. Who were still inspire. You in their magic land of supramental commitment.

14-08-2007 night. 10:00 p.m.

BIRTHDAY SHRI AUROBINDO

It is hyper affection Acknowledge day if you are ready to grasp his valuable preaching's to ignore the highest capable insentient It is not hardship to inter, but the polarity not to repel, for that very-very receptivity Mother to incorporate which complete the bridge of inter developed connectivity soluble by (universal) cosmic heart relationship (Academic foundation built up by Her Inner retreat restorations).

Channels are opened from all the resources, it is up to you to pick up

03-08-2007 morn. 06:30 a.m.

SHRI AUROBINDO

He selected—a confederable person- after a long period this earth pray to all mighty- an solo- different problems were faced by peoples in and out, on solution was seen between war and peace an Angry image was full filled among all other images throughout the world. vital and beautiful love and immortal love become dream.

HE came here and inferred every heart either negative or positive, Dev and Danav and new how to get freedom from slavery intactness of Birth and Death.

It was real approach by His great Spiritual books who concise His truth full effects is a Divine travel from MAN to Insect, supramental land.

08-09-2007 night. 5:30 a.m.

SHRI MATAJI

She is more brisk and extra Cali bared Divine personality involved with exterior and imperial Development of Human characteristic to resonance The true self in encountering with diabolic forces, Inner and outer imbalance of Both good and Bad Evils finally draw forces of higher self to command the static Lower consciousness to evolve with her desire to eliminate the darkness till the super Human appears for further higher approach.

All of us should disallow induction of destructive elements, as She forwarded occult invigilators beside our social inabilities we can not save our self with the solution of soul purpose of main target has been found in very clear vision of Inner Aesthetic world.

11-09-2007 morn. 06:00 a.m.

SHRI MAA

I am too much evident to the god, Who survive me if its bloomish and blush experience innate in all of you grows.

19-09-2007 morn 6:30 a.m.

SHRI AUROBINDO

My profound and obvious contribution to the world → must represent every people where God's desire inherited, vibrate and concentrate to every cell of Body, mind, Brain, and inner outer orbit to full fill Ground and Sky necessities, transforming Man kind- on the way of Golden opportunity.

13-10-2007 morn. 06:00 a.m.

SHRI AUROBINDO

He developed the past (in envelop) in a divine sequence prohibited presence Inverted to the Golden Future in the light of Supramental coverage of Huge Universe.

Let the God converge the destiny of cosmic- Rhythm towards Astral Desire of Great personality who already surpassed his lot of Births involved with courageous Heart to find out the solution of super – Human.

16-10-2007 morn 6:00 a.m.

I LOVE YOU "GOD"

After words- It remains –

I Love You

It travels to the every plane of

1 mind 2. Body 3. Brain 4. Soul- up to micro cell and unit of time— let it cross the every type of emotion affection involvement finally carriage and every corner of Egoistic investment up to "I" is not demolished.

"you" covers so many stages of relations with elements finally It not (Remains) Ruins.

Only "Love" Remains imposes to spiritual diversion and which is Beyond DEVINE and that is SUPREME.

21-10-2007 morn. 05:00 p.m.

SYNTHESIS OF YOGA

What process we follow of love and peace through "HEART-PROCESS same has been envisaged in the "Synthesis of Yoga" to under gone for further climb...... awakening of every step should be adopted.

When this book works on the level of worship then It's Bylaws are comprehensive and Extensive to Devine.

15-08-2008 morn. 05:00 a.m.

Independence Day

"ENCHANTING"

A very receptive feature to present with the country's welfare to eject freedom to different slavery consequences.

How ever "His Project" was begun from this Happy birth predominate days to fill profound truth and piece with harmony from his learnings and preachings. He never mind of what Indians were following before but precast different theories and ideas then follow because, Him Aim is to determine truth full efforts and serve country with honesty and earnest power by full fill dream vision Agenda earlier seen by his in different moods and situation in different meetings and convocations and meditation also. Impersonal and infrastructure of future golden Age. But to understand with higher consciousness only.

You are the person if selected to apprehend provisionally and impowered then It's direction conveyance ways will achieve Aim.

First exercising outer inner mind, body, soul, to make capable all circumstances to produce country qualitative quantitative indorsed mentally then develop inner consolation of each civilian to work as a Agent of Chaitya- inabilities aspirations on the way of supremacy InTouch Ent then every desire of god will enforce you to bring this country to develop in all direction and become guide to for welfare of whole world in bringing Super natural power of supramental- Historical theory Insource of determined prerequisite prayers and Sadhna's tips of great MAHARSHI and MAHAMANA mother thoughts in respect of BREWNING for mind to prevailing soul.

It's very relevant thought continue throughout the day then extend.......

16-08-2008 morn. 05:00 a.m.

THE MOTHER

Penetrating word into Enthusiasm of full Diversion is the principal of mother she is interlocking recline true love to every Roaming Heart, desirous to climb the Hight of in course grading of consciousness.

She always invite attention those who are ready to change and integration required to achieve the target prevailing truth & Honesty **poverty** is not the problem – lively hood of intensity always attached to mind to unable them unchanged and absurd accountability.

Rich in the sense of common majority they are persons thinking and doing and interesting interacting always seeing omniscience and omnipotent vision of life journeyed to emphasize enlightened object always.

Her Agenda is very clear project your self to the Hight reciprocal to the Earth moving to the conversion of broad innovation of mankind is the illumined base of Universe- Velocity.

19-08-2008 morn. 06:00 a.m.

PROJECT OF MOTHER

Sufficient Time is given to in block the experiences of assessed spirituality ⇒

To restore the memory of inabilities and go Forword accordingly, why the object is misty? Desire must be concreted and advised to hold your breathing for a while you are not strong to become silent and witness to observe your self.

Always be in connectivity of mother's respiratory endorsed total incumbency factor of visual intensity of laurel convinced maturity. Be aware of object already conceived stepping the **Time of invent** dream already seen in consultation of contemplation and Inspired focus of segregated secret Project of True Agenda.

21-08-2008 a.m. 03:00 p.m.

SHRI AUROBINDO

Be practical in doing and feeling "His" sovereignty.

Every movement is precious to his memory to divert joint manners. Of thoughts recycling throughout mind in a right direction of spiritual enforcement light.

"His" integrity must be spread up throughout the space.

24-08-2008 morn. 05:00 a.m.

"OM"

"OM" is only your. Righteousness Governing obeying object of your prone prospective life's Era.........

06-09-2008 morn. 07:00 a.m.

SUPRAMENTAL ERA

Golden- HIT is the Destination of this "EARTH" – perfect integrated consciousness is the TIME ever Invented by supreme is Nevertheless true substance. Arrogated in FUTURE.

08-09-2008 morn. 06:00 a.m.

MOTHER

How influence take's place when we come in contact with mother's consciousness:-

1 Each consolation with mind wisdom and command tissues is provided with soul's emission light and awareness.
2 Dazedly and sorrowful conditions indecision have firm desirous inclination with sufficient energy of mother's blessings.
3 Dynamic power will show the right way to step of ahead for your man object and preservations.

4 Your inner soul and chaitya Indemnity Bond will then commanded for inspirational SADHNA.
5 All the bad elements and scoundrels will be removed then occult power will decide your direction in the light of mother's Agenda.
6 Secret Energy will in force- in the proper right choice of supreme to get his insolation evolutionary sect ness transformations process of Human resources prevailed with.

14-09-2008 morn. 06:00 a.m.

SUPERMAN

History player the rule of the nature. it is the god head monastery which ever decided to employ the desire to every sacred mind and wisdom to do the things and thoughts, are decisions then taken in the right time the secret mission is already doing his job according to Determined oath.

15-09-2008 morn. 10:15 P.m.

PUDUCHERRY ASHRAM VISIT

With a upgrade- purity ⇒ you visit that- promissory honored true light broad conscious empowered sacred place and pray for blessings and envisage surrender – in constant silent cohesive instance each moment enveloped with mother's conscient energy always inspired every spirit of this consoled- Earth's Resides.

26-09-2008 morn. 06:00 a.m.

DIVINE

A touch of Divine will reciprocate the Desire in right direction but the consciousness of these powerful –

Erectors and transformers only inspire to those- knowers- who may aware with the real source of- consciousness that may be- from readers, Shdhaks which approach to Mother's Desirous source.

29-09-2008 morn. 06:00 p.m.

MOTHER

Work is going on- some where It is intervening in the middle –

Mother - She has so many ideas, and they have been developed in the different cell's of superior mind – so planning is quite well and up to mark. But the working hours of her project are differ according to – readiness and proper caring of bewilders, so it depends upon- obeying and Governing different outer and inner propagations liable to Divine powers.

29-09-2008 morn. 05:15 p.m.

AUROVILLE

Actually, it is "HE" Dreams through the eyes of Mother, prospected into Divine lovers of Auroville.

further it is best utilization of intelligence first, creativity next indulgency, will further co-existence with Soul to analogue Supreme's Desire in stepping ups and upstairs till the object is found to the accuracy of remark of Her Agenda.

03-10-2008 morn. 04:30 a.m.

PLAYGROUND MEDITATION

I found as under:-

Redemption of occult forces towards – Divine love with marvelous integration to the earth mother endure cultivation of process of Descending & ascending Energy.

Inward transition is- It's core building up receptive towards mother's love incorporating with real enforcement.

22-10-2008 morn. 06:30 a.m.

GOLDEN GATE

It's real Aperture given to you- to open yourself every step needs balanced get up and starting torque to emphasize the Aim towards main object.

Traffic Signals are- subject to deep consensus as and when your requisitions approach to inner voice then convert to Chaitya inabilities.

A long path is invading crossing your age and Time.

To full fil the abilities required for this inbuilt Higher approach depends upon how prayer's approach from heart to heart as per great Mother's convened forces- which needs every cell and soul of every follower.

Every end is beginning unless Golden- Gate opens.

23-10-2008 morn. 11:00 p.m.

THE MOTHER

Earth's unanimous – difficulties and salvation with delight full- efforts just like theorem discovered with answerable doctrines formulas- and their solutions ever searched with the eye of Auroville integrated love rediscovered at different countryman's livelihood to find out the Supreme's Divine at the heart of implicated different minds and wisdom utilizing them for Golden- Future.

19-11-2008 morn. 06:00 a.m.

MEDIATION &CONTEMPLATION

(MOTHER'S CONVINCING)

It is her mystic Approach & determine mediation & contemplation and depends upon involvement with her consciousness and it is for common people somewhere but as for as follower's concern it depends upon man to man.

There are three true views select ONE.

1 personal exotic integration.

2 contra vision

3 acknowledge of real Concentration.

21-11-2008 morn. 07:15 a.m.

MOTHER

There are some- enrich and power full elements in the meditation but activated by Mother's valid concurrence actually, what you imagine for particular sentence which is formality silent but emotional practicing when involved with deep concentration then it is powered and open it's door of bright light.

With search your Inner being that is practical meditation which is fully involvement of Great Mother.

24-11-2008 morn. 05:10 p.m.

SADHNA

Let us have confidence and stable optimistic idea on the why adopted- with some density of pure and clairvoyance, for the cause you have being **brought to this earth**.

Let this flame ignite at very dark corner to achiever- Main Aim have been kept and assigned by Inner consonance.

09-12-2008 morn. 07:45 a.m.

ON THE WAY RELICS FROM SATNA TO PANNA

Dynamic energy- prevailing your heart-needs to compel your whole being enticing in "HER" presence and "HIS" consignment ⟹

Dwelling forces work with your piece and calm presence – combining enormous consciousness and your deep consensus – all the contents of your body cells and Inner being- work as a unit to involve with deep desire and pray to get "their" **Bliss** to find light & Love universally then constrained **mist** is scattered an gleam of prosperity Blooms & cheers the Chaitya invocation.

10-12-2008 morn. 05:50 a.m.

GOLDEN -MANURE

Golden manure is empowered in all the acceptable circumstances your's internal condition depends upon what are objectives- digestible for-that life of earth which reciprocate with your desire and indulgence with One-ness.

12-12-2008 morn. 04:50 p.m.

LOTUS OF ERA

O My God.

Let **His embrace** consciousness- a wake the world – of enlightened awareness- groomed- delight and fired happiness- immortal capability will entrust the humanity of disclosure content of Golden opportunity- Let the **Lotus of ERA** Bloom the centenary of universe. Rectify the transformation technique imposed.

18-12-2008 morn. 05:00 a.m.

THE MOTHER

All the creature of this Earth responding with their own Ideas- Engraved with sectored calamine- Mind and lower insourced brain out of then few are solicited with God's Emergent documentation however mother's province sector calibrate followers Aim, coincide with target of Her Agenda in response of- Supramental Age coverage Huge Humanity an particular time.

depends upon- How few deep representation and invigilators active plans immigrates each follower with mother's desire compromise with Integral – Yoga impowered sect ness and egoless Efforts- brings conscious to higher and higher plane and digest sir Aurobindo's mission of Golden dream – as It is without contemporary Image and any mixing commodities.

01-02-2009 morn. 09:00 p.m.

TRAINING PROGRAM

For training program- at centers:-

Fleet diversion of follower's mind to be ready for future us planning of Mother's- dilemma to consider Autonomous joint reverend of Golden ERA.

Workshop practice to Deepen consciousness for higher grade to meet out the man Him of devotion and clairvoyance as mentioned in the Integral Yoga of Shri Aurobindo's philosophy of true vision with Supreme's indemnity

02-02-2009 morn. 11:30 p.m.

PSYCHIC BEING

Predetermination with flat Idea makes your consciousness gradually up ward – is must with will full effort to elect your Trainer "Psychic Being" who guide your fully spiritual life- will carry to the main Aim- of Splendid Supramental Age.

07-03-2009 morn. 06:00 a.m.

SHRI MATA JI

Her –

Calibration based on profound truth- She was convinced with tackled problems of this earth so as to reach this aspect that everybody should conceive about piece and collaborated love with her blessing after practicing with his mind body Intellect as "HE" Governed her soul's contribution for Integral Yoga with Yogeshwer Shri Aurobindo's Attribute with people of this Earth for supramental intensity of Golden ERA will be convocated in future everybody deserves for transformation and tranquility.

07-03-2009 morn. 06:45 p.m.

SAVIRTI

Conveyance of integrity of this “Monument of spirituality” – Savitri – is spoken language of solicit with Heart opened gate of- prosperous flower of Lotus Impact of seven chakra’s and “Purshottam” Stairs of peak emerging Humanity to the Holy Supreme.

18-03-2009 morn. 06:00 p.m.

TRUE GUIDANCE

Real life chemistry Depends upon sovereignty and History of synopsis of Bewiled Nature in in different births at different levels of consciousness and pattern of prosperity and working ideas,

Preserved at your – mind and Pranik awareness target the Higher object do accordingly with the superior intervention.

Dynamic Divine power exists with your soul. Captive adjoined capability that is your true Guidance in spiritual adopted life.

23-03-2009 morn. 06:00 a.m.

SHRI AUROBINDO RELICS

If you visit the Relics of Mother and Shri Aurobindo – It administer your consciousness to register your whole mental as well as physical categories to involve in the progressive Harmony of spiritualization.

it is not like that Tourist which entertain mind and brain induce happiness and other reverence purpose.

Consistency with the Integration to the Integral Yoga is totally difference than visit of tourist places of Historical beauty Hill stations or other different interests – you should not join all this places as a same as you imagine.

Rusticate your all considerations which done lift your consciousness It does not serve purpose.

Be honest to every word of Mother which dialect your inner Impression and compel your soul to catch interrogation of innovative contribution.

Time is Gold to convert Supramental indorsement with the main Aim of Yog Rishi.

24-03-2009 morn. 02:00 p.m.

GRACE

Ambitions all always expedited to Receive correct judgment for Higher object and activities are follows- accordingly. Be hope full for present will cast past and Impress future pray deeply with Mother to enroll grace for your work and Aim, Be happy always & cater the demand of occult power inspired by Mother for inbuilt Guidance.

04-04-2009 morn. 05:00 a.m.

ON ARRIVAL OF SHRI AUROBINDO TO PUDUCHERRY

Distinct remark (word's) by- Beloved Mother-

Forth coming days will Be full of warm consciences to rediscover "His" Promoters towards ways of "TRUE VISUAL DREAM" At every corner of BEING TIME is responding at Moments of Higher and Higher planes of connectivity of Renovation conducting- rejoice collaborate meditative Best Results evaporating by supramental waves. To every MAN and followers Injecting mission.

You should be very attentive, interactions are caused by illumined mined to impose Mother's Agendas ⟹ "prosperous piece Dynamic power, eternal aspirations flowing through Chaitya commodities – coming nearer increase Receptivity by flowering your heart towards every preaching of Mother and subtle- physic contemporary environmental pleader Shri Aurobindo's consolations.

Prejudiced cosmic consciousness towards MAIN PROJECTIONS of SUPER HUMAN by LORD.

These illustrations are mean to reserve every followers deep "Kios".

01-11-2009 morn 06:00 a.m.

SHRI AUROBINDO'S AIM

Worldly affairs are judged by incorporeal events happen in proven state of trends, we are the instruments are doing accordingly.

Almighty always Desire—for every live to establish peace first then to know the happiness which drives every cell in a correct manner as it should be in the farm of decentralized cycle.

Breathing techniques : controllers your every action of body, mind and soul. That is system of meditation which forward every effort towards spiritualism.

We are required to follow the instructions, preaching in a form of Books, Inner feeling Aspiration but fixing Aim that what we ready to desire to meet out demand to awaken our capacity, over self to find out the Aim to know understand, follow with the eye of inner soul, inner mind, Inner Brain clairvoyance and farther find our every calls to rebirth "God" which is really needed in this Golden Age. Purposely Aim of Earth documentation by Maharshi Aurobindo and Shri Maa in the direction of Super man affiliation with Enlightened Antics.

03-11-2009 morn 05:00 a.m.

SHRI AUROBINDO

It was old Traffic formula to follow up further innovations to gain required Heights.

Krishna consciousness Abroad by Shri Aurobindo introduced to Highlight man object of New Era with total evolution at the New Horizon with the Earth, to console the indulgence of Spiritual consideration of New-Man eligible Discoveries of supreme Desire through **two Great Souls** of Present Age to overcome all the difficulties of proceeding of Golden Globe – Formula of whole Universe come under one Roof with all dimensions and solitudes.

Intervention is Required between the followers of – Auroville to high -jack the main mission of Shri Maa.

15-01-2010 a.m. 02:30 p.m.

SHRI AUROBINDO

It is very benediction to explain the words of Shri Aurobindo – He is redefining the origin of destination of spiritual contemplation of words which are well dressed with illumined purpose, Interpretation are always configuration of settled and cultured mind and brain.

So situation is total different, you are interring to the land of consideration with ethics He is discovering every thing with Elements of wordily consciousness with permission of Greater -Soul.

17-01-2010 morn. 05:30 a.m.

SADHNA

Eyes—cumulative effect is long-lasting every visualize and non visualize object is ascertain action will create thought of aesthetic world, think in a series of different angles where you perform in a direction of Aim.

Mind, brain and wisdom must be involved towards knowledge Spiritual content ethics comes from the origin of Whole –being, when your every cell of body, mind and brain always pray with heighten consciousness –

this all comes by indorsement of blessing and grace of Great Mother.

your approach must 'Honest Desire' and "Diverted mission" of ecological aspiration accepted by "Soul" and confirmed by Directive steps of Inspected "Divine Chaitya" will be your proper Gide in all direction.

Important is living unwanted thoughts and capturing every composite thought come from viable word of Mother and Shri Aurobindo which is invested for the Golden Era and supramental commencement world.

Time is assurance confident patiently perceiving discovering that Higher-peak from where every Man adjoining commemorative transformation "object" of elemental indemnity (Era) Discourse of Human Life converging 'Age'.

watch on your self is the 'key process' before that you must step of Gradually with – prayer of every opt and left Quality of Errors and constitution of different built up effects and efforts then experience lastly Being with your Inner conscience and feeling Blessing and Grace of 'Mother' is the contemporary Reward of Divine and Spiritual Beautiful Life.

24-01-2010 morn 06:45 a.m.

PRAYER

O Mother,

Let me full fill your breathings shift my feelings to the HEART.

Scoundrel ⟶ interacting uphill's may sworn in the light by your— grace provide all being destination avail upstairs it innovative gratitude.

"Focus on widening consciousness

First"- disintegrate all other desires except prevailing truth of your life.

"Reinvestigate inconsistency with Heights. of provocations."

24-01-2010 morn 11:15 p.m.

PREACHINGS OF SHRI AUROBINDO

You must Digest--- orientations pf preachings of Shri Aurobindo and his Broad analytical considered object to identify "Divine" clematis enforces---

Enthusiasm of MANKIND. and Spiritual immensifying prospects emerging in the Energetic field of Illumined Body, and soul converging towards Supreme.

04-03-2010 morn 06:15 a.m.

LORD KRISHNA
AN PRAYER

O Lord Krishna,

Affix my application of your tender probations. Let your aspirations Aware my whole being towards Truth and Love.

Consistency with your power and Light consider my Life for virtual commanding under Shri Aurobindo and Shri Maa's Golden Environment of Earth's mission.

09-03-2010 morn 05:45 a.m.

SADHNA

Modesty Service is required – towards Divine Evolution your mind, Body, and Pran should react with linear action of your consciousness Broadly influenced by spiritual content powers.

False illusions must go, Empowerment of majestic Honesty towards 'soul', must come for further uplift.

Call and call for the Light and power of Mother must approach to the every cell and corner of Heart is utmost important.

Peace preservative consultancy stately will Govern whole --being.

09-03-2010 morn 04:00 p.m.

INNER SADHNA

"Sovereignty prepares (Soul) specific for exhortation; God's mission undergoing with Shri Aurobindo's faculty.

You people must know understand invoice to ascertain whole process of **Inner-- Sadhna** and occult provision of stairs of spiritual content visibility to divert mind, body, and soul ready for transformation of individual and whole Earth with Mother's condensed desire of Universal

Auroville's commemorative vision and Supramental Endorsed supreme Device".

It's Time --bound Agenda with sacrifice and Intensify multi – Dimensional efforts.

04-04-2010 morn 07:00 a.m.

SHRI AUROBINDO

On this very 'occasion' (on arrival of Shri Aurobindo to the India) you must pledge your deeds for HIS PATH was made for total freedom form inner/outer obstructed illusions here clears Raj Marg towards Higher peaks of--- all derivations of Supramental Age of Golden probations.

24-04-2010 morn 05:30 a.m.

SHRI MAA

Her Words—not only explaining but adjoining your consciousness and inflecting your device.

Watch your self with three angles.

1. Honestly
2. Inwardly
3. Firmly

Modify your Nature with desirely pray to mother what exactly necessary for you – In 'God's Hour. it is Real fate of immortal Lively hood and Spiritual contemplation.

Always present in 'Inner conscience' will inspire for presentation yourself before Bhagwat-Muhurt is most Important and unveiling Considerations.

26-04-2010 morn 05:30 p.m.

SADHNA

Soul—conscious device may bring you to the desired path of Sacred. Land further will entrust for consideration your way towards peace and prosperous Life will enforce you towards. Aesthetic reward of Provision in wisdom Intellect sources at **chaitya** confirming contemporary desire to meet challenges from --- Interferences and confronting device by Dominic forces, to enter that Divine- consciousness which impulse --- Higher object towards Supreme Desire where Ascending Descending Takes place with Handling probations of Mother's invocation's Allocated concern.

SHRI AUROBINDO SOCIETY CENTERS

We have gathered hare to counter Balance—Blooming's records of society centers engraved founding's Improvements and entire after effects with efforts of desirous implications in different matters gestures we should never forget --- Mother's confederations for evolutions How consciousness spread up to capture resolutions and applications Mind, Wisdom, Intellects—cover prospects of Man to ready for transform visible Aims and directives of Shri Aurobindo to bring Integral-Yoga in a Real form and clear concept restricted discipline Informative object and Time bond declarations Should be purpose full and concrete.

Results must come out see that—Past envisages, Present encouraged and future cultivates the soul purpose of main objectives of Supramental Age so discover your self and surroundings endeavor the Divine Consciousness collect and pray until the Inner conscience locate your participation in this "YAGNA" actively Honestly, Investing whole Energy for which Shri Aurobindo and Mother dedicated God Hour Always present awake your self with truth full efforts.

SADHNA

Monotonous Resources all to be removed.

Your main Aim is virtual to the soul comprising device.

So whole being is contemporarily visualizing Suprema's desire as if other contradictions or provision of Resistances to be kept apart.

Do as per inner conscience deserving for --- Mother's Great affirmative Divine preaching's as targeted towards Shri Aurobindo's mission for Time bound transformation Installed on Basis Golden opportunity. probation is always on the base of subtle physic ("Suchhm-Bhautik") Amendment shared with universal desire of God.

Indian mythology and European concept is unprecedented – by Shri Aurobindo while searching spiritual content mandates, with his super-consciousness so attributing the broad minded formula, He always Inspiring aesthetics judgment without favour with Binocular Concept of "tatasth-tadatmya" Insoluble Refractive depth of Heart comprehensive effort.

09-07-2010 morn 04:00 p.m.

SHRI AUROBINDO

"He" (Shri Aurobindo) is garnishing 'Truth" to the soul of every Devotee against that false-hood which arrogated outer -inner space of Person.

It is that effort of species where everyone Should alert with his "Main object" throughout HRS for that very phenomena Bhagwat Muhurt respond If he has receptive power and urge with quit and Love.

Disturbing elements are always trying to abrupt your consciousness If it is you Grasping Energy and Let the consciousness come down Lower and Lower against that Grace which is showring power and Light, so every moment is the mater of Supervision and Alertness.

Scanning your mind, Brain, Body, Cells Pranik aggravations, Enrollment – your Whole being in the Register of Higher Mission of God's Abbreviations to prepare for Mother's Achievement of Brighter Divine Soul.

You should not absent but your Presence in Higher Peak, will be presence of consciousness which involve a Group of Devotees for victory which Signals to get opportunity become supramental indemnity in Light of promising project of Golden Beauty ever not seen, but- Experienced by – **Two Great soul's** of Spiritual world Inflamed and shined.

10-07-2010 morn 06:30 a.m.

SUPRAMENTAL ERA

It is notable to every Devotee ---- Maa and Shri Aurobindo they are indispensable undefined approaching through carrying of that dialect where every spirit of spiritual world head Divine—conversion who pledge kinetic Energy under guidance of clairvoyance whine every path of forwarding motion is cleared through exact prayer is made for him and carrying mission of Earth of her call for "Maa Bhagyati's consensus".

Future is convening present will be forcibly handled.

Past was promised physical, chemical and Bilateral Elements of Nature are enhancing their power on Man. Inductance of vision in the multi dimensional Enforcement will bring transformation.

Man has to be changed in the Hight of Supramental Era.

11-07-2010 morn 06:30 a.m.

SADHNA

Supreme has Instinet through Mother—Bifurcating **His Desire** commencing Spiritual environment --- had seen poor condition and lower consciousness at the level of destroying whole infrastructure of Earth and Humanity It is very indigenous to over come destruction and bring Earth and Man upward and to render His Eye as Universal confined vision of Love beauty power, Relevant authority of **Vigyan May Lok** so as Bhagwat peace. Will work and Earth will transform along with live and non alive Elements.

whole Compendium will speak the Language of **SUN** and His Reverence of Rays will Absorb darkness and Allocation of all type of Assault and Dignities of "Daitya Powers" will be diminished.

25-08-2010 morn 04:00 a.m.

EVOLUTION

Supramental resources were opened to envoy all the calibrations of different mountings of Mind, Body, And soul—to the Persons as Supremacy Desired Interior decorated aesthetics of people and superficial decorum of outer world must enable to achieve intellectual performance of whole environmental atmosphere of Earth, so that Love get all freedom form body and engaged to Soul --Conceived authoritative Administration.

A new shape of ERA will sworn on Earth whole consciousness may accountable to Supreme only and Supreme Desire may be counter part of whole universe, than only "Divine" Placement of dynamic Energy will superb to the super man for transformation.

Goal is High---

Man is slow---

Consciousness is step by step, upgrading **MASTER** is with full dream vision of Lord.

Past is Reciprocating Present is converging future is Engaged for transplantation of mind, Body, soul, and Heart, Time is Ageless, sympathy is full, Accepting Grace and blessing are rare, but Subtle- Physic is Assured in full swing for Golden opportunity for conversion to the Earth.

03-09-2010 morn. 05:00 p.m.

SHRI AUROBINDO

You can not understand "Him" with aforesaid –(site) sight.

His works are mirror- to adjudge "Him" and Integral- Yoga"-

Bestowed- cultured thoughts contain to superlative consciousness adjoin your desire to in block all the possibilities of evolution of "MAN" for goodness to this earth- this Brand Spectrum Idea in heart the Heart to Lovable piece and wisdom then It goes to know and understand the God and his universe, then mind get freedom and goes to real source of innovative Reserves of present Age. Till the consciousness goes upward.

Shri Aurobindo enters to those mind, wisdom Intellect and Heart- who have real sense of opportunity of God's HRS" and goes to the mission of attribute undivided consciousness which search "MAN in the God".

Ultimate truth of Supramental inabilities to every "Soul" will transform this Earth.

17-09-2010 morn. 05:30 a.m.

PRAYER

O Mother

Let the competency restore back the situation.

Find out appropriate person who register the preserve and control the prophecy and acquire the piece by renovative efforts.

24-09-2010 morn. 06:00 a.m.

PREYOR

O supreme

Carry me to that- conferring area, where only ⟹ Divine surges exist.

29-09-2010 a.m. 06:00 p.m.

INTEGRAL YOGA

Human psychology- cultural heritage- systematically- buildup the consistency to the person further liquification from of personality works- accordingly we are people of gross implications of mantel, physical, ecological, logical, environmental, critical, abbreviations, by different births, and aesthetical contribution of chromosomes and chronozones.

Entire energy needs to be similar initiated integration of hypothecated thought of polarization.

AIM of Integral Yoga adjoins – total Identification of your's authentical – "Awakening of every cell of body and soul's contemporary enduring Supreme's desire of deep SADHNA as indicated by our "Sadgure" and gratification of "self"- ego. Then surrender reveals Real personality to meet divine priorities for further way as- inspired by supramental synopsis of spiritual intensity device.

30-09-2010 morn. 05:00 a.m.

DIVINE VALUES

Dear friends-

Find out-

Divination of consciousness by custodian reverend relay: and-multiplication of higher consciousness by inspired able authorities

Deduction of – invading and aggressive atmospheric surrounding.

Sum – of – all the enduring capabilities of receptivity's by study preachings attending large scale reliable intellectual spiritual confers meditative enforced – conductive grace Aspiring induced SRADDHA.

Then abstract must by comprehensive Vigyan- Mai- Anand Mai-probations to install the- Divine values of golden instinct Era of the Earth.

30-09-2010 morn. 06:00 a.m.

FOR MAGAZINE AGNISHKHA

GUIDE-LINES

We must focus on ⟹

A- Stamping of the new generation – towards Spiritual indemnity.

B- Feed back from the different findings as such-
Organized spectators of different localities through out the world.

C- We must analyze the devotees and their steps towards transforming stages of mind soul, body,

D- Unprofessional directives must be presented so as to reach to the Aim of supramental spectrum of Golden Era.

E- Questionnaire must be brig up an update recycling of precaching's and Sadhna's in response of Brilliant directions of un-contrary vision seen by Shri MAA, Shri Aurobindo.

F- Reconcile the – whole spiritual journey of different gradings of SADHAK'S or devotees may indicate How Bhagwat muhurt consisting their enormous true Self desire – Resulting condensed Divine object towards new probation It should represent – Reliable resources of Integral- Yoga people concern- magnifying Aim of Shri Maa- It should mirror of devotes in the transparent credible form, (all the lamination must be uncovered)

22-10-2010 morn. 05:00 a.m.

MOTHER

Bisect- The centrifugal force of the Energy- towards soul consciousness you will find spiritual Hight which generates Divinity though out the HRS.

This constrained enforced power is likely to be engaged your whole being with Mother's consensus Her preaching's to forward you in the right Direction to visualize the Aim to overcome the obstacles and to involve with the supreme consciousness with the prayers as need from Time to Time.

You are the person if one selected for the cohesive enthusiasm and spiritual enhanced- mission- then you will feel loneliness with collision of every atom of your cell as needed upper stage blank will conceive with the peace but you are not alone mother is always with you with love and Grace.

You go ahead- some body is waiting your approach you will not tier till the Aim is completed, then you will adjoin with "Vaiswik- Chetna" afterward to full fill the object. Your call with emerge your prayer will emerge your soul will emerge then you will be submerged to the Integral consciousness of Super- Man inviting new Era to transform. The Universe.

23-10-2010 morn. 05:45 a.m.

BHAGWAT MUHURT

Himalayan- comprehensive atmospheric and Environmental aesthetics is a sacred Heart of spiritual identities. They always appraising aspirations and guidance under supreme powers. Their allocation and systems of preaching's are improving Sadhna as required by different organizations and individual depends upon what they require in the field of upgradation of spiritual words so as to welfare of whole Earth and it's real requirement.

Universal Enforcement Energy has to be cross different obstacles made by Occult Forces.

Gyan, Karm, Bhakti, depends upon- conditioned sources of different births. Position of today is apparent individuals. Desire new united in the direction of false, wrong, Doman, Dark, collective consciousness now bringing Down ward this Earth.

Every Soul of Saint converging from Love, Light, and Beauty of Supreme is working in the Shape of Different power of RISHI in the real sense now has clear vision of clairvoyance and intellects to Improve the present condition of Universe.

By means of descent and ascent and their provisions in the SADHNA by the desire of Divine- AVTAR to complete the object of subjective KARM of how God shapes the Man in his consciousness depend upon the, TIME SPACE, CALL, DEVOTION, GRACE, & BLISS of MASTER of the Institution and faculties.

Allocations are available in moderate form (terms and conditions are very clear) JYOTI is ready to enlighten you Bhagwat Muhurt will take you to the mount, ARE you READY? only is the delay in the farm of centuries and centuries............

24-10-2010 morn. 05:00 a.m.

GUIDANCE OF MOTHER

For Before Sleep-

To the meridian of as apprehension of consciousness to the magnitudes of spirit is obtained- such night- mares are allocated at the different provisions of DREMS to determinate of finding correct guidance his necessary.

Sympathetic guidance of Mother may be called bay prayer deeply.

These HRS of night are approach to the divine path if executed right procedure of spiritual consensus.

For your Intensive Extensive object- your intuitional mind must work in the Night throughout HR.

28-10-2010 morn. 05:30 a.m.

SADHNA

Remember: earnestly your last breadth experiencing prefixing your tenure to the High profile adjective – **KARTAPAN** will vanish-

Trace your whole being inviting pleasure to the every call getting in touch with Divine coloring connectivity detachment with Lovable object of premier consignment,

Aspiration, Grace, Surrender, Blies are your objectives in the Direction of Spiritual life feel always you are with Mother and her subjective support with clairvoyance – retaining Integral consciousness to follow the superior Aim of Golden Geomatical ERA.

Power full your body mind soul, to grasp the Ascending Light and figures the same to enlighten the subjective source of your ailment-

Freeze all the embodiment Desires Let them evaporate your desire of supreme will appear when Beauty of Love to cover your Heart then Immortal Every- “Paratper- Bramh” will transform you the divine concern Intrusion.

29-10-2010 morn. 06:00 a.m.

SAVITRI

"SAVITRI"- is the God's vision ever seen by Shri Aurobindo in the 'Emptiness' and 'soul' consciousness – but the paradox reconciliation must adjoin advent Truth will consider every Man to open the every knot of last end from where by rebounding we may reopen the apparel of birth's intoxication by celestial improvement to reach to the Aim of Evolution.

You breathings are there for initiations specific words may prolong your SADHNA by heart to reach to destination In dreamed by Maha Yogi and Maharshi work allotted by Maha Bhagwati organism.

07-12-2010 morn. 06:00 a.m.

MOTHER

THIRD Power: you have, but you must unitize for contra vision and comprehensive achievement of your self.

Six Sense: is meant for (Utilize) innovation, and concealing true substance. (chaitya)

Impower: your mind, body cells, emerging Soul to Divine involvement.

You must know your "AIM" no compromise for any self- enjoyable things.

Your are for- MOTHER, of mother and must acknowledge Her preaching's. Every word is stair of mount you should be very clear – for your adjective and total accountability for "Her Directives- Time to Time- impulse your heart to get in touch of purity and Improvement of every sector of personal responsibility in the field of subjective "ADHTATM".

So en bloc your other Interests and Let the Love knowledge beauty- flow towards- Mother's fourth Dimension's Resources-

What exactly – It is dream of AURO-VISION, TIME is Gold not to waste more.

Awake your self know there is: nothing personal to impair Every undivided is cosmic caveat to achieve the "GOAL".

18-12-2010 morn. 04:00 a.m.

IMMORTAL DIVINITY

Immortal Divinity – Rest upon conservation of Energy of call center.

You must breadth in Lentil Position to over come all the difficulties of Life.

There may be circumstantial trance inherent you for Awakening your self Through the HR.

Every outer communication of demand & Rescue – carry you to the sufficient distant of Bhagwat connectivity.

You must pray for best of affects in the eye of Vashwik Chatna as needed by spiritual confirmative Subtle-Physic.

How ever it is should not: you are bound to regret any desire completed in the wrong direction your search of Aim (must) inhale in the true Direction if you are on the way of Integral- Yoga by mean of Mother's councils primitive efforts and Shri Aurobindo's incarnated reinforced comprehensive Divine activations.

You must signature on the well- by bringing your pledge to consign with the transformation and Innovation as & when require by "Chaitya-Purush"- Because you have come for the same you live for the same you devote for the Highly Inflammable Agni as Heart needs to improve the man object of Shri Aurobindo's mission.

24-12-2010 morn. 06:50 a.m.

SADHANA

Let the primitive forces – visualize the desire – Supramental consciousness is perfecting Browsing & compelling Souls of the Earth to the context of the reference we. Are the people adjudge and adjoin the Bhagwat- Muhurt at the cost of our repulsive forces how magnetize the Lines of forces of Rishitwa- Jagran Available Awareness Influencing

Innovation and transformation by In during provocative compulsion by Supreme's Desire.

Insure that undivided consciousness plays the vital Role in the Field of- purity , Love , prosperity, Beauty, and- Infor cement of undivided desire towards – Aim of Shri Aurobindo's & Shri Maa How they dream the MAN towards Brilliancy of transformed superlative Mountains you are person to process the Vidhan of Prakrati & purush and change the universe to Immortal True Substance embroidery new wave of Golden- Age by fire the empired inner consciousness of individual's "Time" is always embarking you.

08-01-2011 morn. 06:00 a.m.

SUN-PATH

Inaugurate. Your self with proceedings of Mother.

She is convincing your heart for proper guidance and duties towards responsive authentic efforts to highlight the Aim of Integral -Yoga do accordingly Be always positive In Thought maintain harmony by mind Intellect and soul to determine object of different preachings delivered though different media including Subtle-Physic provocations are always to join Vaishwik Man, Pran, and Soul including ethnic body.

Unprecedent reward blessings and print of foot step are always there but It is need to adopt directives as It is without your mind and intellect then visibility will be very clear with different objectives of eternal consciousness reciprocate deep consolation of mother she invite you for Sun-Path to adjoin the Immortal Enumerative substance will Bloom Golden- Flower in the Futuristic- innovations.

She has shown you the Search -Light of past, present, and- provision of Auroville's observations.

It is your responsibility to adject the- Dream- Vision of Supramental-probations.

Be ready with prompt- accountability and Enlightenment of whole being to Accept every momentum pressurized Subornation to adjoin the Time-Zone of Bhagwat- Muhurt, Insuring main survival certification of Human-Technology's superb.

Time, call, Pray, - will change whole Earth In peculiar manner as desire by Supreme and you are the target they are the cause "Adhyatmik Utsarjit Shaswat Chetna ke kendr Bindu" then total will be recycled affirmative and Imperative contemplated Universe.

11-01-2011 morn. 06:00 a.m.

SADHNA

Reu- Mpire, the your's Divination to the soul impower the Aesthetics of Spiritual Identity to the mother and her object insuring that you are proceeding and enduring true Element considering your visible prospect of Inner consciousness and confirming real **I,** Body PRAN are on the way to Divine- Path you must have exercise always that God is undertaking you in every prospect, work Done by body, mind, and soul and you are not the object, but **He** is presiding everything at All turnings then you will realize year whole being under his considerations then Chaitya- Chetna will take over the mission of all objective by Enforcement of Shri Maa & Shri Aurobindo's collective- works and proceedings till then- you pray for Blessings on each step of Integral consciousness how-ups-down take place till the realization of confirming your transformation and Divinity ready to adjoin Vaishwik- Chetna emerge to the "Whole One" Emblem the Truth with Suprema's Signature.

12-01-2011 morn. 06:00 a.m.

SUN-PATH

Replenish Desires are counting new starts, Be cautious perceive the thing how happening to your being Inter link the different Abbreviation takes place you must see the distinct object.

Eyes must know the real vision of constraining consciousness towards perfection of Sadhna how ever your all parts of Body including cells must be in a linear position with mind, body, and soul now you are on the different mountings and leap towards ignition of brightness of Light go ahead .... Go ahead on call of every voice follow the path of sun only......... glimmering of Light house ..... is coming nearer with the Aim of encouragement of Supramental Resources.

12-01-2011 morn. 09:00 a.m.

SHRI AUROBINDO

Intuitional: micro observation has been put up by Maharshi Aurobindo to determine some other facts which were not lighted by other earlier observers, not It is way of Intellectuals but It is a Refined classic observed clarification by clairvoyance, geographical zoological Historical chronograph was total surveyed in the field of spiritual content figures by Shri Krishna- consciousness finally chosen and brought to the plate form of Universal consciousness in the form of integral- Yoga to enlighten the supramental consciousness to disfigure the Demon forces and Victory to commence new Transformation of whole personality are total Sterilization of Human Converting Earth in new Era.

13-01-2011 morn. 07:00 a.m.

MOTHER

We are the sun of – Mother should have positive- Approach adjoin with Accountability and works and (Inner) consciousness must see anxiously aspiring at great mission of Inner-circle of Path finders with truth full efforts systematic plans indulging Aim of Refreshing every cell of body for devotion you will get Bliss and blessing of Mother pray for the-

(God)

O Brilliant- Accordant commandment of Every sector of Body, mind & soul may response to mother. I call for light - & power o supreme.

17-01-2011 morn. 03:45 a.m.

MEDITATION

What is prediction of work predetermine me to cons tile to the object and definite the mind, body, to soul continence vision to Light Hight the Mother's descending process inviting for colorful way to spiritual Identity confirm.

Let us revive and Hold the mission pray for Sinusoidal concern with intensive meditation to ascertain forward step Chaitya- Chatna to Vaiswik- Comprise combine.

01-02-2011 morn. 05:30 p.m.

SUPRAMENTAL AGE

All beauty of Life: is renovated through integral- Yoga.

Elementary knowledge of spiritual content fixture with ancient features and modern technology – was combined and studied with deep Intension of knowledge and meditation techniques- finally inspired by soul Awareness Integrations It was Resulted into a super Human complexions determined the power, Light , and Aesthetical Improvement finally adjoined the Aim of "**transformation**" of whole Universal Lives – A new Era may sworn, with a new volume of multi Dimensional umpiring and innovation of Supreme's Desire in a Golden Stream of supramental Age.

Auroville is an ever event of new Approach to the cosmic man- kind.

03-02-2011 morn. 05:00 a.m.

INTEGRAL - YOGA

O Team, Leader:

I bow to THEE. Let me ignite my desire towards- path of Divinity Shows Imperial touch of Love recognized by Supreme only.

Insuring believe, accountability sovereignty devotion and blessings in a single room of greater opportunity, Leave all the thoughts of other Directions leaned regarding thoughts you should be selective ONE DIRECTION- ONE AIM, ONE MAN ONE DIVOTION your whole being should be brightened by SUN of destiny- towards transformation – pray cell for Bhagwat- Muhurt is Approaching have a perception of truth of your Life for soul deserving connectivity to invite

Mother's desire to your every cell charged for conservation of regard you must have clear vision of "Internal-Yoga" decide and conform that you are on the Path and conversion to the **Chaitya- Chetna** offer only- Light, power, to Cary you to the "New Golden Age" still-ness is required to serve the purpose.

27-03-2011 morn. 06:00 A.m.

SHRI AUROBINDO

Intervening soul with body He guide to understand true Vision of Life.

It is spectacular conversion from static energy to Dynamic Energy ever Done by Shri Aurobindo Through His SADHANA.

There are series of steps between mind to wisdom mind to soul mind to body and mind to supreme to Lighten the "object" HE has made Bridge of clairvoyance without Interference of knowledge of written statement of old and new testament or RISHIE'S ARSH-GRANTH.

As per Directive of Lord. KRISHNA Divine Status was cultured it human stem by bringing. Supramental Grafting A "NEW MAN" is Sworn in a cosmic world of spiritual Identity by Impowering Light Bless Light, Bliss & Grace of confined Maa- Bhagwati He was success to struggle against Demon powers and brought a Victorious new ERA. In the Aura of Earth. Brightened.

Encircle His preaching thought your mind to upper soul till the wisdom and knowledge is converted to the faith trust and surrender.

you have to work hard when celestial touch of enforcement of your desire consume your full energy and all resources of Divine consciousness project to the only mothers Desire then you will able to – reach real approach of Shri Aurobindo's dream vision.

Receptive reconciliation of whole preserved BHAKTI is needed to serve the purpose It you are ready then "Bhagwat Muhurt" is recalling without delay

31-03-2011 morn. 04:30 p.m.

SADHANA

You rapture this Silence and preserved it. It recalls your compound structure in all sense towards soul's Awareness.

It is miraculous condition when you stop talking watching discussions and any meeting with other's except spiritual consensus atmosphere, maintain this Integration till the Hidden agenda achieved a Glance.

09-04-2011 morn. 06:30 a.m.

SADHANA

Liberate your self for consignment.

You are collected hear for disintegration of your those Habits who full fill your other desires rather then what mother Desires Each and every involution contains – some purpose How to transform your different minds brains Hearts adjectives and Let them coincide with Shri Aurobindo's what exactly his mission collaborate with- agenda was made in different preaching's and inspired by clairvoyance. these informal preservation my convert your that idea which is not progressive.

Hence you are required to – insure encouragement of you works and efforts How you can first achieve- peace, Actual silence, and inward all the briefings of mother, every thing is presence except of you – open hearted criteria to involve the fire to ignite your self and brought before BHAGWAT MUHURT Concentrate your whole being towards rising SUN of supramental insource you will become part of undivided consciousness reaches to the goal of Integral-Yoga. As this Earth will witness new ERA.

11-04-2011 morn. 04:00 p.m.

SADHANA

After long awaiting you have reached to this "Stage" to refine you consciousness and consistency with mother's Desire.

bring all of your different objectives to the one platform of "Peace" to recognize your self the way form where this journey begins to Adopt relativity connectivity, sincerity prominently truthful efforts to adjoin Sadhna's mountings.

Loneliness comprising your undivided consciousness to adjacent the Aim as prefixed, inspired, and kept to determine your adject way of spiritual commitment in this birth.

To accord the permission for the cross the different ways of darkness are different imparities. To ascertain that all of you desires inflames and transform to the way- when, mind, soul, and body- emerges to attend, in corporated object of subjective enforced creativity of mother's installed desire - you pray, feal with heart go to the divine consciousness when it permits to open way to connect with chaitya evolution is the premier object first form where- all the ways opened to go forward with HIS efforts to redefine your birth for supramental objectives which are very- very whimsical and convergent to the way of Shri Aurobindo's objects.

27-04-2011 morn. 05:45 a.m.

MAA BHAGWATI

Listen to me:

Warriors of this struggle must be your – self commodity go up to that point where every desire mee to your one demand. Primitive involvement of Integral- Yoga Maa Bhagwati insures you to reach the destination your outer and inner journey consumes to Higher consciousness your visible object will be indispensable soul Awakening.

27-04-2011 morn. 03:15 a.m.

SAVITRI

This is unwritten agreement to cross the bewilder cosmic world and to reach your real state at every part of your being.

An musing touch of Divinity from Static to Dynamic conditioning of mind, body and soul and to superb experience of Different level of consciousness up to Highest plane of Divine world to introduce your self and spiritual basics to deepest Illumined powers to inaugurate the suprema's constituency of different travelling's of man from birth to imperial immortal end.

29-04-2011 morn. 04:50 p.m.

SHRI AUROBINDO

When "He" describes many secretes of journey for Integral- Yoga as such Different steps of spiritual content opportunities – then he is entourage His Brilliancy and intuition through your heart then it goes to your mind and brine it is sure connectivity such great Yogi which is directly involving you to the Supreme's divine touch.

05-05-2011 morn. 05:15 a.m.

TRANSFORMATION

Your job card endure sedative approach must be to enhance target make visible so as to confine your consciousness upward stairs till the object is completed and another mount is seen evolution is mean to cover your whole being as suprema's desire tally with the what mother corelate with her Agenda.

It's the Earth's prayer in oriented to the SKY- Target of Integral – Yoga and same is visible as Shri Aurobindo's concept of transformation of people and Golden reward of MAA- Bhagwati.

17-05-2011 morn. 06:00 a.m.

SADHANA

Ultimate Truth: is to compromise with your conventional powers to ignite consciousness towards illumined mind, brain, and body.

You are here to import all your inconvenient receptions and Inert your soul's main, contemporary real approaches then specific Silence and Peace will be preserved. It is the base on which you will do all efforts of spiritual convections and reach to the ultimate target as mentioned at Integral Incitement ever seen by Shri Aurobindo and Mother as approached to the Devotees to complete dream vision of Auroville and Golden ERA, consignment was clearly done as happened by clairvoyance at subtle physic's dynamic evolution of Divine powers.

17-05-2011 morn. 06:00 a.m.

FOR SAVITRI

To conceive the Truth → words are not to be contrived.
Impower your →
Connectivity with Soul observing capabilities not your knowledge.
Inner consciousness always receptive to the Heart's condolement.

"Be Aware and Awaken – when you perceive this manifested and evolutionary sacred in volume also before and after study.

28-05-2011 morn. 06:30 a.m.

SADHANA

To anchor the Hypothesis -- you have to work hard you are at that point of configuration where every portion of your mind body, and brain is on perception and every turning will show you, your mirror of Aesthetical element

Virtual quality to be improved and you will be feel pleasure and Happiness as you proceed ahead according to your Internal consciousness than what step is chosen that will be best.

31-05-2011 morn. 05:00 a.m.

SOCIETY- CENTRE

Corrigendum: of every Society-Centre is needed to be - perceived It should not be left on his beckon and Let and Let if carryon without improving his captive energy, power and innovation as per mother's Desire

Society are Aashram of Pondicherry and their Executives are devotees are mean to take oath to divert to everybody for readiness for transformation not to ignore Aesthetics principals preaching and devotions for which Shri MAA, Shri Aurobindo have cultured divine power to elaborate every creature costume of present body first in crystal form then up to dissolved by Integral -Yoga, to Identify "Himself" to know what is their Goal and effort in convergence of Astonished Supramental World to entitle the Aurovill's object and subjected appearance of Anandmai, Bigyanmai, Truth full Nature and projected works, advertisements mission activities to convert man to superman in the real Science as illustrated in prayers of mother and what abjectly She desires from you and your institution's aperture.

Overall responsibility goes to Shri Aurobindo Ashram → How – consciousness Spread up throughout devotees and shape up the project of consignment between Mother and their disciples or devotees as per Agenda because time is recalling Bhagwat Muhurt is Present and every in absentia will pay cost of invocation and accountabilities.

05-08-2011 morn. 03:30 P.m.

SADHANA

It is very aforesaid truth to identify whether you crisp your consciousness to mountains or live as It is.

So premium thing is – enhancement of diff. moods to the Integral-Yoga and know your exact path. To opt and efforts to reach the destination until you experience the difference of now and then.

All and All is deliquesce of Approach where all the circumstances meet to the Bhagwat Muhurt and cause of you life is relativity with your self and soul's connectivity here approves to divert whole consciousness awaken and surrender comes to join mother desire It is true- self Sadhna is required for all devotees.

08-08-2011 morn. 05:15 a.m.

PRAYER

Q profound mother,

Let the Golden -Lotus Insist me to awaken the whole being, persisting immune cells enlighten and transform the existence.

09-08-2011 morn. 05:00 a.m.

SADHANA

You feel: cosmic volume of the soul:-

You will determine – possession.

Will understand deep- Inner consciousness-

Knows the faculties of SUN-SHINE.

Do the efforts as "HE" – desires.

That is the Primary "GOAL" for forward Action to Suffix. Mother's Attunement, and Agenda.

"You should come out from the viscose attachments"- abruptly.

15-08-2011 morn. 11:15 a.m.

TRANSFORMATION

It is an extra ordinary and self explanatory device, which includes supper natural derives concluding part of progression required for most update Sadhna in Spiritual Content Bhagwat Muhurt – It helps to inward Integral growth of consciousness to forwards you towards mother's Agenda and Shri Aurobindo's further consensus to heighten impact of transformation.

27-09-2011 morn. 11:15 p.m.

SADHNA

Incumbency to individual contribution of mother's Agenda is lagging behind.

We have opportunity to make than able to determine the path of Shri Maa but consciousness of continent is not ready till new Let us find out:

The System by which:

Our preachers or some of the devotees may love login there mind/ Heart how deeply connectivity to be made perfect :that each person keep first step.

a) deep study of Shri Maa and Shri Aurobindo's preaching's and Literature.
b) Search there on way to take next step of prayers and knowledge extensively increases as required.
c) Awareness about his mind, brain, to accept the consensuses Integral- Yoga and resect that knowledge kept earlier of different views and ways as he met with different persons or book in past - is vain as per his Internal soul.
d) As receptivity he gains he may go forward for farther steps of evolution.
e) What we have done what we are doing and what to do is to be acknowledged.

01-10-2011 morn. 06:15 a.m.

SHADHNA

Mata physics is involved in human physiology and quantum theory of static- Dynamics whole cells tissue of the body ate working on the basis of worldly Universal -Soul – How It cares with the Spiritual tactics and your different births, mind, brain, soul, wisdom and cultural- Genetic Heredities.

All these are projections of different fixed four dimensions were sworn from Time to Time.

Think tank are both- Doman Divine forces their fractions and developed shapes in a Human resources.

They envelop the Humanity in different working Phenomena, some are slaves some are Dictators and some are Administrators in different counters.

Now days "wealth" is the Diagnostic developed currency, powerful hijacking all the Bed elements **ASURI- Brattiya** is impowering **Prabhutva- Satta** on the greedy person on all level of consciousness lower and lower they want to register their presence in the different fields-security, Agriculture Education Health and other relative fields.

Omnipresent and omnipotent faculties are developing their---Resources—Through different spiritual forces saints, SADHAKS, prayers at present.

We are the person of Physical Mental Psychosomatic, having ANNAMAY, PRANMAY, MANOMAY Bodies- Abilities :-

Needs to be transformed first in a peaceful tranquil shape then deep theory of inner Consciousness works

Ahead:-

How ever meditation takes shape after long strong desire, If people needs to be changed as per his “SHPADDHA” Govern. By soul-connectivity till awaken by MAA Bhagwati takes further Charge to discharge the Impurities and Indispensable desire of supreme then Govern the SADHAK.

We are the lucky at present to be SADHAK How ever Bhagwat Muhurt is present all the resources of spiritual contemporary are here brought by MAA and Shri Aurobindo.

Asper evolution MAN may ready to go to further new- Age. But It should be desire of average to enter in a Golden temple---- for Transformation of Consciousness for a Super-MAN.

05-10-2011 morn. 05:30 a.m.

NEW-ERA

You are given whole universe to opt?

You are thinking of yours It is widely form: of Consciousness you are required too.

Improper residual convince. Are there.

You desire for:

Speak Listen, See, Read write and place your self under the Installed capacity where brooming -love wisdom beauty Ecstasy blooms--- through your whole being by educations preaching's. Aspirations prayers---- efforts by mind's convocations faculties different Consensus enlightened powers and Light to Heighten the Consciousness up to the mark and Visualize the golden dream of transformation.

you should learn Practice diversity connectivity, Receptivity to impower you self to adjacent the Aim of Mother's Agenda with Peculiar goal of Earth's dimensional Approach of subjected discovered desires---- How Shri Aurobindo carry different objectives to the front of **MAA- BHAGWATI** to bring down **New- ERA** to from PARTHIV- JAGAT to Immortal- JAGAT it is a Bristol -Regard of clairvoyance with Subtle- Physic.

17-10-2011 morn. 03:45 a.m.

FOR UTTER- YOGI BOOK

1- It is trillion technologies of vast spectrum of spiritualism.
2- It is very Interceptive conception of the Life eager to grasp Higher convention aver seen by **Utter-Yogi** in the Divinity process.
3- The **will** which confirm all the dignitaries of mind and wisdom reciprocating True- Substance of the Inner Consciousness.
4- Arbitrary Truth has been Glorified in **Utter-Yogi's** covert.

22-10-2011 morn. 05:00 a.m.

GOLDEN-AGE

Let us Revive unto the Path and Glory of Mother:

She will rebuild and consider as per your surrender that how receptible organs and parts are intended to serve the Mother in real sense—depends upon spiritual Intensive collaborations earned in this Life and allow you to Identify your self and know the destination towards way shown and adopted by inner and outer orbit of reconciled—spirit Consciousness of Ascending and descending constitution of Shri MAA and Shri Aurobindo to Inter to the Golden Age.

08-11-2011 morn. 04:45 p.m.

WORKING-PATTERN

Whole work is being done on the charter prescribed by the Shri Aurobindo on the basis of Adjective synopsis of Integral-Yoga at the analog of past findings and present Insertion of vast integrated Consciousness.

All the Aimed concerned devotees should work under collective Consciousness but "**One**" should know his responsive readership steps to kindle the object of this spiritual mission which is yet to be done.

All the allocations, Institutions are their dividends followers of Divine Paths should know the accountability Responsibility to come to gather to serve the purpose of "Mother's Agenda" in real sense.

Time provides you Bhagwat- Muhurt in the sense you should exact the clarified purified transformation objective. Till the surrender comes your inner soul confirm the way of Chatiya-Chetna How come forward to take you to the visual prospect of **Golden ERA.**

13-11-2011 morn. 05:00 a.m.

INNER CONSCIOUSNESS

It is very vast induration ever in the History – How to imprint- knowledge in the Heart – always questioned by argumental hypnosis and tactics first determine the fact hat all the inner collaborations of the Body emblem he transformed entitled process of conversion – spiritual concession whole cells divined Consciousness enveloped by suprema's desire than what you see--- superficial contents in the Body is not?

Yes: But the affirmative Spirit of console invoke the outer orbit of Higher Consciousness.

Hence you have to perceive by inner Consciousness It is not presumption approved by old ethics or Religious Book or predictions but real Fact is --- Imperative and superlative- omni science will bring you the – omni present confirmation by soul's connectivity emphasis that HE or SHE is not simple or common MAN but is constitution of divine- supreme, which you have not yet identified by integrated Consciousness.

By all the Installed capacity of your's whole being to the self-Realization then uplift to the front of mounted true- element then you will – impower and know and understand the Gesture of phenomena with consultant of Inverted Wisdom and knowledge.

"Real Receptive acceptance comes by Heart's concise knowledge not by mind, brain and wisdom.

18-11-2011 morn. 11:00 a.m.

SHRI AUROBINDO'S DIRECTIVES

These **forty years pd** (with discontent features) was specific attention towards Destiny of **Earth** ever prayed by **Her** in distinct Dimensions. Whole was conversion of perspective future of MAN and It's volume by integral-Yoga consigned.

19-11-2011 morn. 06:00 a.m.

SHRI AUROBINDO

If you are broom of universal soul then it will renovate whole being in the Real sense in all respect.

Shri Aurobindo was inspired and attributed with mother India and climbed Top then see the Inner/outer orbit of conservation mentality spiritually and physically and know it's constitution and development of infrastructure of MAN and His cycle and whole environment of Earth.

An Brisk in content brought Him before supreme and supramental organism then vital force converted to the Divine content Energy than invited Golden promotion of whole universe as per resolution of Higher convention Super Age.

20-11-2011 morn. 04:45 a.m.

SPIRITUAL - CONSCIOUSNESS

Every thing is presence, nothing is in past and future.

It is ridiculous to say that past is present and future is present.

Present is your whole nervous system circulatory system metabolism, Immune system and whole life style. It is required to increase receptivity and connectivity with the **Love** which is present always.

It is reciprocal with the Aesthetic ethnicity but you should aware and awaken with soul's responsive Intensity and Integrity.

Spiritual- Consciousness is viable to the Heart's- Accountability and Heart is persistent to Inner collaboration since different births and karmic-accounts to adjoin knowledge and Bhakti in the real sense.

Make convalescence relationship with your breathings there IS Harmony of peace and fire at a glance.

Witness whole thigs with your Inner Eye only. You will only. You will find there ocean- of Love and that is Supreme.

02-12-2011 morn. 10:30 p.m.

SADHNA

Input your all the—regards and aspirations to the collective-Consciousness to emblem the source of spiritual Consensus to the people who are on the Path of Shri Aurobindo and Shri Maa. let them trust and awaken the heart to consider the fact that object must be obtained with in their ability and approach, what the intuitional upper conscient may adhere the Integral -Yoga to Heighten the Man.

Your purpose is to make them in a royal touch of supreme- Love to reach to the Goal of Mother's Agenda and Golden Dream may sworn.

14-12-2011 morn. 06:45 a.m.

SHRI AUROBINDO'S COMMITS

It was dogmatic and constrained experience ever shared by Shri Aurobindo at the desk of similar equative concerned person or Sadhak with commemorative resource of inner Consciousness and impersonal wing these who are willing to invest their fire of knowledge they will imprint his custodian preaching's thought heart and will acknowledge every prayer are mantra as may be their own installed wisdom earlier.

Awaken your inner outer orbit of consigned PRANAGNI, let it Ignite your combined system of collective Consciousness of Integral- Yoga Who will within your Sadhna throughout HRS.

On very vigilant and Hostile Honest to Impregnate the weavings of Golden Dream. You will find your self the meaning of your birth in this association of Auro- vision of transformation.

09-01-2012 morn. 05:50 a.m.

MOTHER

Mother:

She has developed Science of concentration, converted to meditation in every Effort.

It was Her contribution to the Humanity- over Rule on all type of Evolution till now where everyone has perceived his progressive-possibility in one species, She has developed Whole "Vikash Vad" impowered by terrestrial Love, and Esteemed unlimited capacities in the mind, brain Body and Spiritual contentment acquired by each cell of Body.

She was Immortal Divine- conception of transformation of Living JEEAN and is breathing to the each devote at Past, Present, Future and further becoming revival routine up to that period till Shri Aurobindo-Dreams the Golden opportunity converted man to Super Man in a deliberated Stage.

This Earth may take shape of Auroville.

25-01-2012 morn. 07:30 a.m.

SHRI AUROBINDO

Subtle physic has been conquered Esteemed truth has been converted into Divine.

It was certain phase of "HIS SADHNA"

God's premises was sworn in Bhagwat- Muhurt.

Old tavern was Sympathize by Veda's Upanishad's and Gita and New concept of "ANAND" is Built in the Supramental- Core of cosmic Consciousness.

This Earth has Seen Glimpses of Supreme in every soul now it is Return Journey till Divine conceive in the every cell.

28-01-2012 morn. 05:15 a.m.

SADHNA

There is way to wake field --- synonym to Identify the fact that after acknowledge the spirituality every moment is Judgmental, you have to exercise more and more with clarity of knowledge and mind full efforts.

Do as you can find your way to go insight.

23-03-2012 morn. 11:00 p.m.

AUROVILLE

I an going with such affirmative efforts – that Divine convulsion will witness this Earth ----- Human has crossed his limit of confined elasticity of past. Ingredients and ascertained his dignity of evolution.

Mother's still response of concrete solution of "ONE World" and "One Consciousness" and only "One Race" has been magnified to the Magnitude of decentralized Humanity only deserving to SUPREME with the eye of HER Agenda may sworn NEW ERA of Golden Age.

Welcome ---- Supramental authenticity of Maa Bhagwati now taking shape of **Aurovill** at every Hearts of Devotees.

20-06-2012 morn. 06:55 a.m.

SHRI MAA

What is hidden Agenda of Mother?

Concrete solution of Human- felicity towards growth of mind & wisdom and complete environmental-comprehension of transformation of Earth for Supreme.

22-06-2012 morn. 11:25 p.m.

SUBTLE-PHYSIC

For whom you came here?

To invite ensoul elements and inner conscient and work upon different objectives of MAA.

SHE has blown you and empowering for integrated consciousness to full fill heartiest desire of Shri Aurobindo to bring sown Bhagwat-muhurt in which man can mirror him self and ready for new Amazing faculty where God-Head HRS weave super mind to influx superior decoration of new Earth with interior-incarnation of subtle physic of suprema's Breathing sky star-lit.

26-06-2012 morn. 06:00 a.m.

MOTHER'S AGENDA

It is Arbitrary-truth that we are upon to Shri Aurobindo's commandment why should be not: collective movement towards one consciousness with one Leader ship establishment and first one Agenda-convertible prospects of every soul my carry that mission towards Light of Enlightenment then only second step my eligible for further height.

It is to- remember: mother wants to bring you on one platform where you are ready made parson compromise with "HER AGENDA" by unknowingly & knowingly grasp her consciousness and grace may insist you for objective decision of Shri Aurobindo's declaration of- Incoming Supramental-corps of Golden Age.

10-08-2012 morn. 06:00 a.m.

THE KRISHNA

The Krishna: The Divine Invigilator.

Because of you,

He could erode true substance of human resource to convert the whole- being and accelerate the further development of Earth.

Valuable 'soul' to command the body, brain, Intellect, mind in such a way that newly Internal consciousness is ready to accept the configuration of clairvoyance of entitle KARM, GYAN Bhagti surrender the inspired soul of Shri MAA & Shri Aurobindo and their Aesthetic movement of inner world to come under the coverage of SAT. Chit and Anand. The moto of entire Integral yoga. And evolution of Auro-contentment ever perceived by mother.

03-09-2012 morn. 06:30 a.m.

SAVITRI

To comprise may be less, hard or typical, but to precise is not so simple.

It is like to climb without claim

"consciousness" travel at the level of mind, brain, pran intellect since different birth.

but "He" has crossed the limitation of whole being All allocation of different planes of mind.

Savitri- may not be counter file at the level of even spiritual- identity.

It is vain to transpired or interpretation at different levels.

Very body wants to Zoom.

Mother was first and final ecological mirror of this scientific research of spiritualistic-claimant.

It is not matter of configuration at any language.

It is only "Pray" to determine "God" at the level of consciousness according to devotees as they are.

and consideration by Shri MAA and Shri Aurobindo only grace and blessing works at the dignity of egoism & surrender.

It only blooms in the "Heart" and tonic to reach supramental heights at the cost of how fire accelerate and become "yaggagni" for Ahuti as per clairvoyance of great allocator of heaven ever seen by Shri Aurobindo in the "AURA" of whole universe.

08-09-2012 morn. 07:50 a.m.

SHRI AUROBINDO

Shri Aurobindo Ghose: was enormous gesture of supreme, owned by him sworn as Shri Aurobindo further (completed) contemplated universal consciousness spiritually attributed consolidated consigned Divine Power interrogated IONS of Declined Ither with Illumined magnitude diverted to TEJUS- BODY.

Let the BRIMED- present combined TRI-CALL- occupy
supramental manure enlightened whole Earth-Venue.

19-09-2012 morn. 06:00 a.m.

YOUR-ROLE

What is **Your-Role** in this Ignited Integral Yoga.

An Eminent promotor of cognition truth which reveals a vast majority of Real Devotees.

As how to surrender to An Agenda Manipulated by supramental Discourse as Perceived by Mother It-Self.

18-11-2012 morn. 07:00 a.m.

MOTHER

Mother always perceive you should know to ensure of gracing and blessing to receive her in consciousness of opportunity given to you.

Read, know meditate the words how works to abject your heart in and out of your whole being.

Observe throughout hour where you are and where you are not.

Innovative- Efforts of Mother works according to your attributed desire.

03-01-2013 morn. 11:00 a.m.

SHRI AUROBINDO

He is so derived – person- that He has opened him self for All wishful organized, devotees to well understand that he has owned that path-which will reach to the highest peak of innovative truth, love, humanity Honesty supremacy, Divinity Finally cross Boundaries of spiritual continuity reach to the Supramental-Tower from where Dream of Superman Become true.

21-03-2013 morn. 06:30 a.m.

SHRI MAA

Reveal the truth inside- you.

Preserve yourself (with) against evil forces.

Mother is Always- Awakening your sleep is long this is the time where future is knot, past is preventive, present is very-very authentic Age of Renovations Identification and cultivations of old. Ethics bewilders are on.

Death is compromising Redefine energy towards-higher peaks where golden Sun is shining and soul consciousness is inert with Heart- flowering Love light, spiritual identity with descent immortal coverage towards Divinity.

An Supramental energy is covering whole cosmic Rhythm each and every soul is decoding Affirmative proclamation of Golden-Age by two great costumes of entire clairvoyance theory and doctrines now taking shape as per shuttle- physic experienced by suprema's Regenerative sources.

01-03-2013 morn. 07:00 a.m.

SHRI AUROBINDO'S CONSIDERATION...

Appropriate Situation to influx the Inclination with Shri Aurobindo that is core impairing first with determination of his path ignoring other derivative efforts so as to reach destination in such a way that where mind, knowledge acknowledge the configuration of Divine values of whole being.

It Should be very clear that Time Zone of shuttle physic is playing important Role despite considering different slabs of undivided- soul's consciousness.

Insure that you are going straight way of sun -shining.

You love him with honest approach of mind body and soul.

20-03-2013 morn. 05:00 a.m.

MAHARSHI SHRI AUROBINDO

Maharshi Shri Aurobindo is gospel pray of super dyne ever done for innovation of earth it is proper channel connecting terrestrial world of spiritual identity by Broad-Band.

The Mother: consolidation of mind Brain, Intellect, body, of soul by integral yoga for identification of super-man an living jean contributing device of heaven at every individual of cosmos.

These dynamic forces are energetic for every nucleus of heart for conservation and sublimation KARM, GYAN and Bhakti.

Creative transformation is the motto of 3rd dimension to reach the Aim of vision of Further true Subjective world.

Omniscience and omnipotent waves are covering Earth for awakening Human's physiological Anatomical and Spiritual Stages.

28-03-2013 morn. 06:00 a.m.

BOOK-"GITA PRABANDH" BY SHRI AUROBINDO

This is Epic to involve with Insisting Authorities of super natural powering "One" who loves you.

"Gita" is sworn through KRISHNA- consciousness by shri Aurobindo.

It is proverb of Generalization for spiritual Impact of every Soul.

05-04-2013 morn. 05:30 a.m.

SHRI AUROBINDO

Shri Aurobindo: has called upon to listen him abruptly, to impart his collaboration of Divine Manuscript to surge his immortal weavings for subjective Incorporations to bring truth to your mind, brain, Body and soul for consideration of whole coverage of Human Cycle further Innovative-participation of Physical Mental, vital, planes, to heighten uptill upgradation saturated to his findings as per his directives and dreams projections.

Console your self, your being to universal-Soul energize and awaken deep desire so as to reach to the- call of whole synopsis become dedication of whole being form where HIS- JOURNEY begins evincibly.

03-05-2013 morn. 06:00 a.m.

AUROVILLE

Auroville is Non conventional project Insisting Non Racial Humanity Astonishing a world of conscience through Mother's Agenda by togetherness of Divine Soul in the Divine Body It is meta physical concept of suprema's Vision.

It may not repeated contour.

08-06-2013 morn. 06:00 a.m.

"GITA-PRABANDH" BY SHRI AUROBINDO

Bloom reward of the "God" ever obscure.

Divine consciousness Travels to convert Entire man's crimpling desire with his whole being to install- Heightened Divinity with acknowledgement of Spiritual content vast knowledge to know the Real Karm, Gyan Bhakti and advent the comprehensive Enlightened soul.

02-07-2013 Night. 08:40 p.m.

PRAYER

O bloomed Mother:

Regenerate my thoughts of apparel to Divert to Soul Consciousness Throughout HRS. Let the Light impale on my whole being through your grace.

17-07-2013 morn. 09:00 a.m.

TRUTH

Relevant truth is always with you.

You have to feal and Emerge.

Do, whatever comes: after depth of chronological Order you opt in a Visual intensity.

19-07-2013 morn. 04:00 a.m.

SHRI AUROBINDO

Beatitudes of whole Body cells-are scattered throughout Universe for anticipated Sadhna at three Magnitudes for transformation of Earth only.

01-08-2013 morn. 05:30 a.m.

SHADHNA IN A CIRCULAR MOTION

You have to divert your full- consciousness towards God's Awareness.

It is done:-

1. By bringing integrity whole being
2. Thought moves towards -Spiritual- Identity.
3. Every desire is thirst of supreme.
4. Every action begins through Remembrance of Lovely concurrence of Divine.
5. Every moment is serve to God only.
6. You Should know:

   Breathing are taken in a cosmic energy of subjective motion.

7. Movement of Body's part takes place by bringing down as "HE" is doing.
8. 'I' Must be replaced by "You".
9. Soul may adject the whole continuity of "cheerfulness" throughout HRS.

28-03-2013 morn. 06:00 a.m.

SHRI AUROBINDO'S CORRIGENDUM

Every cell of Blood must- inhale Divine's Indemnity.

As Shri Aurobindo's corrigendum opt his consciousness of Divine.

Every Cell of Blood was photo- (synthesis) cell of Genetic Technical Theory has invented Real -God- particle (brought inside) was scattered throughout cosmic reverend It has the reason that Pigmented Sun rays were consecutive up to certain pd after **HE** left this Earth.

04-08-2013 morn. 11:30 p.m.

SHRI AUROBINDO

1. Swear your desire to the god eventually.
2. "HE" should be in your eyes, mind, Brain, wisdom, and soul:
3. It's the Ideology- pattern of Rife style Beside.
4. Part all of other devices open in your life.
5. Yor should grate full to "Him" to reach you to this prospective, spiritual, certain higher peaks for further ways of divine curvature identified you among awakened captive power of peal devotees.
6. Pray & pray not to indulge further diversity of compassion and inertia of weigh full condition.

03-09-2013 morn. 06:00 a.m.

SAVITRI

Congregate your- self in the new dimensions of- Savitri…… which is an opportunity provided you in this century.

You are the first person to go through all the way of spiritual content stairs by awareness of mind, brain, intellect, wisdom to get full explanations, expression and derivations before reaching to the mind setup to prepare for Integral- yoga.

Then Rival journey may begin by put up your whole being arresting your desire to climb this Path earnestly by Heart- strengthening to allow the power Light yogagni through direct ambitions resources of Shri Maa& Shri Aurobindo through there advent: caricature synopsis of aesthetic Holy speeches writings and great volumes to eject- spiritual synonyms of old- Sanatan yog and new Dimensions of Integral yoga joint venture, to heighten the man to super man and able to enter to the- fragmentize Door of supramental yug.

To revel spiritual Identity of priority of that period – you are here.

07-09-2013 morn. 08:15 a.m.

BHAGWAT CHETNA

1. Console; gratitude, throughout atmosphere Abeyance of governing powers.
2. What exactly my done for you is being. Your Reverend has being taken and produced before..........
3. You must crystalize the formations of qualities Response for lower consciousness and dark abandoned virtual evince.
4. Every 'HR" is being- perceived and arousing accordingly.
5. Thar are different categories of thoughts and reproduced efforts effects from time to time It needs to demoralize and support according to there goodness and reveres prejudiced matters.
6. What is needed for you **Bhagwat- chatna** has got proverb and adjacent power reserve for light under which guidance: only Mountains are adjectives to resolve fully Righteousness of your spiritual- future.
7. Your determinations favored and powered by "Mother" will only interest you to sky the evaluated task allocated will further converted to different experiences of Highlighted spiritual stairs are permits to enter the specific invoice of deep desires of Maharshi Shri Aurobindo and Shri Maa.
8. So be very- very...... convinced with speeches of Shri Maa further become- power full thrust to go to the path of **Bhagwat chetna** to carry you to the Destination of Integral-yoga.

19-09-2013 morn. 07:00 a.m.

SOUL- CONSCIOUSNESS

1. This overall journey of soul- consciousness:
2. Now it is middle.... Of Adoration and inculcation with the body reproductive criteria throughout the universe.
3. One should be very careful with the Eternal- configuration of isometric- desires of collective consciousness which is penetrating a large Area of cultivating passions diverting Attention of Lower and lower attributing part of mind and Brain with sensual conservative parts.

4. Only anatomy should be indulge with the commemorative resolution of Spiritual console dicers in the field of……purity and spirit- content configuration.
5. Extrovert world is- regenerating the Idea of suicidal- connectivity and Demon forced strengthening resulting- going to worlds disaster.
6. Extrovert- Bifurcating zone is being speedup now beginning journey with God's desire to be supreme in sequence of core empowerment spirit gradually up coming instinct knowledge.
7. Maa Bhagwati has approved resolution:- transformation ma take time.
8. Shri Aurobindo's- Integral-Yoga is the Resolution of Mother to umpire the Man's Journey up to Divine Conversion of exact knowledge supremacy to the experience techniques may appropriate Integral- Yoga to the Enlighten mind categories to heighten the soul to flesh the path of supramental-Age will consolidate the Divine Dream of Maharshi Shri Aurobindo

31-09-2013 morn. 06:30 a.m.

MOTHER

You are enrolled in the basic theme of majestic state of occult powers governed by Eternal profound truth of paramount distinct object.

Roster is ocean of Love and peace throughout universe spread over to indulge with opt and realizing then reckoning.

Acknowledge your self to persistency of mind brain and Required knowledge of subjective accuracy in the Heart.

"SHE (Mother) is confirming desire unto you experiencing to Be and Do Accordingly.

You should ready every moment and caliber with receptive conscience open your Vital-Plane.

22-09-2013 morn. 06:00 a.m.

COLLECTIVE- CONSCIOUSNESS

Collective- consciousness-- is a integral-part of determined, mind focus ON "Integrated Truth" ever seen- when- occasions are organized to proceed with the achieving on the pointed harness with Individual followers are turning points with mile stone to reach the Destination Dreamed by Allocated path of prejudiced Maharshi Shri Aurobindo as Mother always Interrogated in her Aurovill's Predetermination with Future- Come- True of Subtle- Physic.

01-10-2013 a.m. 08:30 a.m.

SHRI AUROBINDO

"His" total concealment of Life was annexure of supreme and considered Him, for Galaxy of Enright power of common people to improve and bring to the Light of sagacious gracious confinement of All- Spiritual Authenticity of Veda's Upanishad, Gita—etc. to combine with Soul consciousness only to give them Definite source of Integral- Yoga to know the virtual Love, peace, power, and cross Devotee's comfort Zone bring to the platform of spiritual Identity, form where Decent/Ascent may Superb and perceive the Destination of Higher Omnipotent, Omniscience objective.

Supramental is the Effort of Grace of Lord, to Bring Heavenly Imprint Innovation, through Maharshi Shri Aurobindo.

Mother is still Governing and Appropriating of Different sources of Bhakti, Gyan, Karm of that devote who is desirous to target His heart for Her Resolution of peace, and follow the grace of Mother resting upon objective of surrender very obviously.

Total is a not agenda any where but god is perceiving Him self by every cell of "Man" to convert Divine Light to Become Son of Every Moon (Disciple's devotion Assignee).

21-10-2013 morn. 03:30 a.m.

MOTHER'S VOICE

As Monotonous sound clearing – preservation from toxication and daring to Imperial perfection on Dividing Sinusoidal waves at linear composition with powerful frequency.

24-10-2013 morn. 06:00 a.m.

MOTHER

Awful- Representation of the "SATWA" radiating cosmic Energy— Emerging Subjective coalition to Superb the consciousness.

Every body needs to --- accelerate the Heart's Empowerment- for Further Innovative truth- Endorsed,

05-12-2013 morn. 09:30 p.m.

SHRI AUROBINDO'S DEPARTURE

Inward the promissory Note to rediculate the consistency of truth of the Earth, for transformation of A MAN and visualize the Aim and Destination ever is the path of Omniscience, and Omnipotent --- the vision of Shri Aurobindo and Recognition of Supreme.

AN PRAYER

O Festive Devine.

You left this Earth:

for commemorative people Inner conscient may contingent, for immortal journey. Though Integral- Yoga and survive for supreme.

08-02-2014 morn. 05:15 p.m.

100TH ANNIVERSARY

(29 MARCH 1914 TO 29 MARCH 2014)

An Relevant truth ever Seen—in the

Golden History – Where two great Soul's- had invent- idioms of optimism classic Hematology, enthusiasm of development of mind, brain, wisdom and body with relative quantum theory and ancient acknowledge of

Vada's organism and Upanishad's creativity and connectivity of objective and subjective orientation of Deep. Omnipresence. And omniscience, omnipotent alimentary projections. Of Spiritual comprehensions.

How consciousness awaken from static worked to Dynamic Representation man Becomes Super- Man Through supramental Resources, Bhagwat Muhurt is contemporary when Mother has played vital roll in the filed of Adjoining people of the universe come together by "Aurovill" and Impower the Dream Vision of the Shri Aurobindo to Highlight the Renovation of "Chaitya" ingredients at the level of higher and Higher consciousness till the Golden -Era objective comes true.

Here is a new Dawn obtains by bringing Supramental Energy to Spread over the Earth to insure Divine -Life- Mission sworn upon universal consciousness.

20-02-2014 morn. 06:15 a.m.

SAVITRI

Oblation this great— grosser implicate- determination of whole being

Towards identification of Lord: at the level of true resources by deep consensus entire eternal governing's from life to death and innovative discoveries of mind, brain, wisdom, and there deviations and different characteristics from static to dynamic ranges of consciousness with will full and unrest consultancy at Divine- Mountains.

For the Followers: He Should signify his elaborated mind, first to accept receptivity at the ground level of wisdom and ready to leave the past preservative life then He will ready in the real sense as mother awoke.

First step is to realize your definite improvement by brining your consciousness from lower to higher applications as per mother's Desire, and ready to study simple trigger of techniques as mentioned in the directive of mothers as per your necessities which differ from man to man.

As per spiritual intensity you will get your Aim, prayer and way of finding your Soul to reach the destination further steps may gradually earnings of experiences adjoining your Sadguru or Supreme.

22-03-2014 morn. 05:30 a.m.

IMPARTING VISIBILITY OF SUPRAMENTAL HASTENING

Psychic – Being is over whelming your Destination.

Peace fully await very earnestly, micro observer are on line- associating at ground level.

Awakenings are always in different steps according to momentum theory of dynasty as per approval of your regard "His" contemplations improving whole being around soul around clock, around body, mind, wisdom, It is restless theory of becoming- "wizard".

follow Instruction of inner being very apparently.

Supreme always confining your desire to Superb Humanity characteristic of gesture evolving with clairvoyance of Maharshi Shri Aurobindo's Dynamic theory of assent and decent up to Divine World of SUN Get in touch of Great MAA Bhagwati and Her Planes.

Everything is happening with and according to Subtle-Physic witness the valuable Remark of "BEEING" and Becoming Best of Humanity and Earth.

23-03-2014 morn. 06:00 a.m.

BLISS

Bliss ---- is awaiting for domination some – whispers are overwhelming due to passions and intoxications regard for prayers is need to reach to the destination where no desire of materialistic word ------ remains although it is hardship but it is simple to convince your stature how to evolve with reachable peace of soul only which is your first aim of considerable consciousness at higher plane.
Let him do leave on him be with his configured empire;

PRAYER

O supreme ;

Let me devote all desires on your,

"One" immersion dilute the same.

23-03-2014 morn. 06:00 p.m.

SHRI AUROBINDO

Even after happening Bad to Worst…. Some **souls** are Being prepared and authoritative for conserving changes and transformation as a whole --- by gracias Informed of great majestic Shri Aurobindo at the level of His condensed creativity.

Every solid Deformity of nature complexity of personality is changing into gaseous and Liquid farm (of Amity) which is not apparently.

Every body is interlocking of Tri call is habit confirming accessibility of security.

Demon forces are on Top. For Distortion on other Hand. Down Sworn at the Threshold of Haven.

These parallel are consumed till supramental overlapping the universal **consciousness**.

Great forces are in invisible will come to the platform as and when requeued by psychosis of cosmic Reverence of subjective Analysis of Discourse given time to time by Shri Aurobindo, when adject the time of transfers conciseness Auroville will invoke at every Sadhak in real sense then "Glam" will convert in to SUN as par Device of Conversion and aspiration of Bhagwat Chetna and Bhagwat Muhurt.

Theory of Distortion is the Subliminal to the theory of Divine Appropriate the Distinct Doctrines of Adjacent "PURN-YOGA" Super natural connectivity of Earth. To Supreme.

26-03-2014 morn. 05:30 a.m.

THE MOTHER OF COMPREHENSION

It is very nomenclature to the Spiritual world it is focus to the interior Decoration of mind, Soul, Body, till the Awaking, It determined collectivity of whole being interceptive of the Love, Light and Integrity to the Divinity.

Always we with the Mother she Has intensive care to redressal for each and very soul to carry to the extreme welfare and Destination for Distinct target.

16-04-2014 morn. 06:00 a.m.

AUROVILLE

Auroville - is Such a Divine Place- Which Reciprocate your **consciousness** - to the dedicated work as required by Mother without rationalization of confirmation of your own superficial mind's desire but to connect you with required selection for this Integral-Yoga in response of your Receptivity and connectivity.

06-05-2014 morn. 10:50 a.m.

FOR STUDY CAMP AT PONDICHERRY

Total pull through- viscous Intensity of **Avatar,** go to the Discrimination design mindful cohesion discussions Reading the theory of different characteristics of what Shri Aurobindo, States intend to cover his Holiness, Broad mind, wisdom, Brain with enlightened words:- and how ever Listener accept and grasp with his own intension.

Main thing is: Achievement of this collective conciseness, How mountains are created to see the Visible Aim are Destination of Spiritual Identity to sever purpose of **Camp** and get objective.

(Hook-up your knowledge with "HIS" collegian crisp).

10-09-2014 morn. 06:15 a.m.

THE MOTHER

What the Mother: -

Persist here-

i. Disintegration from all the Governing body's pertaining to immersion.
ii. Your livelihood to be according to allocation of peace.
iii. All the preservatives of past to be dissolved as seen unfavorable to your Sadhna.
iv. Subtract the consolation of all thoughts denying the path of "Her Excellency"
v. See- Do and do not for the destination fixed as per inner **consciousness**.
vi. Breathing must be organized in such a way that no moment should be calculated without existence of supreme according to Bhagwat-Muhurt.
vii. wait till the awaken of soul then do accordingly.
viii. Inconscient is preparing your foundation implicating your whole being ready to follow the path of Integral- Yoga.
ix. If everywhere is delay is distant from "SUN".
x. You should Embark your knowledge mind, brain, soul, linear constituency of distinct desire of HER motivated Agenda.

xi. Subliminal sources of Supramental coverage to Universe will entrust A New Heaven you will be one of the Devotee if become HUTAGNI of Shri Aurobindo's Art of "Spiritual-YAGYA".

13-11-2014 morn 05:30 a.m.

TRANSLATION OF SHRI AUROBINDO'S WRITINGS

This is vocabulary of Spiritual science developed in a menace sprinted devotion of eternal Art.

You are Interpreting the Ideology of writer interlinking with your digestive knowledge of Imperfection and unsaturated carve of so called Aesthetical world, Identical Technology of your personal vision of Mind, Brain, and Wisdom.

There is quite difference between planes of Hierarchical Dignities Universal Soul conventions—and self Approach towards unidentified resources of self technology of Un visible Art of Analogue writings and their motives.

All above is the: Clairvoyance of spiritual mountains incomparable with surface Games of different consensus of Mind and Wisdom.

14-11-2014 morn 05:00 a.m.

ART OF BLOSSOM

Art of blossom is important:

For that very reason you are required to dedicate your self and reciprocate your desire towards- plasma and Devour It is earnest and deepest that conservation of energy is required for accent and descent both have a tall confidence than grave pray with Mother.

O beloved mother;

How to impower console that every moment convert into follow you way and experience for your great blessings and Krapa to exhale Divine consciousness forever.

05-12-2014 morn 06:00 a.m.

ON DEPARTURE OF SHRI AUROBINDO

Prayer: -

O Maharshi

Your departure is resolution of superb man Kind at the heart to sworn heaven to devotees is total clairvoyance of Supreme.

Let us pray to inflict our Desire in his consciousness and follow his path.

28-02-2015 morn 05:30 p.m

SADHANA

You have been plunged to vital platform of- INTEGRAL- YOGA of Maharshi Shri Aurobindo.

It's a leap after deferent births to a higher object of ever Golden Aim prefixed by related Mother by her blessings and immortal peace.

this opportunity is a rare Divine – Vicinity needs much more efforts with your whole being every end is your begging till the Aim is not obtained.

21-03-2015 morn. 06:00 a.m.

SADHNA

Flourishing the Truth you must know your priorities:-

Detect and Identify the creation and origin of thoughts -Activities – results effects on body, mind, and wisdom there of, concern with Mother and her creation and try to involve with spiritual Directives and Divine sprinkles on mind, Body, then altimetry on Soul, your Destination comes then.

So be visual of daily Routine of Mental creation resulting Physical and psychological – ecology and environment of Atmosphere Around your self.

Your whole being must be very aware and see the thing happening with total calm.

PRAYER

O delight full Mother,

Let me aware of broadening of Aesthetic Heart and concentration to know and understand the True -Associations.

12-04-2015 morn. 06:00 a.m.

INTEGRAL- YOGA

When you come to the- INTEGRAL- YOGA – An Bond is full felled within command area-

Choice is opened on Desire between implementation and Resolution how it takes shape in the future.

So many doors are opened gradually to Empire in the different field of mind, wisdom, vital, towards Higher mountain further transformation

Here Divine aspiration works as per deepen consensus and Desire there if.

10-08-2015 morn 06:00 a.m.

SADHNA

Illusions covering falsehood of life, and vision is hence not cleared.

We must pray of discerning Earning and prestigious embodiment to leave and to get transform in the Divinity.

"Shri Aurobindo has witnessed→By clairvoyance,-- transcendental incidental materialistic and spiritual world and scanned – every individual in this Earth process is going on as required.

Things are accelerating which are Worst and Best at a time fill the Bhagwat Kripa replace the unwanted and place the wanted, there my be desire of **Supreme** in a "Time Sequence".

We know things in outer orbit but Inner is still unchanged.

We decide the matter but It is supposed to be decide by others.

We know the final destination and result, but decision is pending till now, away for accountability of self for which Shri Aurobindo explained widely.

16-10-2015 morn 07:15 a.m.

MOTHER'S PRAYER AND MEDITATION

By scanning the soul to devotees put up to the Divine conversion. Mother carry everybody towards higher consciousness according to receptivity and devotion.

One thing is very important:

She has targeted each and every step of Shri Aurobindo for transformation what **He** exactly dreamed for Supramental-World from that period It is continuous process in shuttle – Physic Diversion of each in a timeless Zone further becoming neared to Chaitya- Chetna then completion of Supreme's Desire for Divine Project conveyed though strong channel of Maharshi- Aurobindo.

17-11-2015 morn 06:35 a.m.

THOUGHT- AN MAGNETIC ENERGY FIELD

- Magnetic field of the Earth is power full and Receptive Simultaneously.

Every Inner /Outer thought is vibrating particular energy – goes to the magnetic field changed with thoughts.

We are effecting – whole Environment of Earth – by selecting thoughts – Right or wrong Finally converting KARM and Experience there of.

So It is not Individual/ personal harm when we are angry but is it universal, it happened in the same way when we are happy converting energy of Happiness to the world.

New days--

We should see our- self what type of energy is dissipating throughout HRS- Further- Negative waves conveying powers of Individual to worldly waves to Impower Dominic forces converting Attributing **Terrorism** every Home is playing Important Roll by investing his energy by

Angriness Occult powers are doing there work in destroying Humanity Man, by weapon and treatise (Shastr and Shastra) in different field.

So we should be very selective in thoughts further creating it's own world of Impurities or Divinity.

So for this very purpose:-

We should ready to perceive our self – Inner and Outer and willing to change, nature built up by different birth – although it is different task but is possible if we are ready for spirituality.

The things will be apparent are not in particular place it they are placed accordingly then world will change – as Great –Mother Says.

If we plan to contribute this world, then only peace may of obscure and only Happiness may subsequent.

02-12-2015 morn 06:00 a.m.

PRAYER

O, Divine Mother,

Let me kindle the desire by your grace to superb the Adjective possession to withdraw the support of wrong coverage.

29-02-2016 morn 06:30 a.m.

DAY OF SALVATION

This the day of salvation when Earth stimulate for carving Her condition of injustice, dividend for the Lack of Love, (Mortality) mortal-considerations going towards Disaster.

This is the day of Immortal Truth against deferent grievances to lift Humanity towards super Human.

This is the day when grant Maharshi Shri Aurobindo's Devotion towards MAA- Bhagwati concludes Supramental power entrusting great Revolution of Evolution bring Heaven on Calvin Earth.

Let us pray for this great Immortal EVENT:-

O Supreme,

Let Shri MAA, Shri Aurobindo Constraining desire accelerate to each Human of this Earth and every Atom become Divine impowering Existence of your's Shuttle- Physic we are a always Great full----- always-----

08-03-2016 morn 05:00 a.m.

DIVINE RESOLUTION

on the peripheral of Earth: Divine resolution of great rishi's i.e., (Shri Aurobindo, Shri Maa) is accelerating executing through their preaching's there is a vast universe and it's Aura – containing different faculties of visual in intensities of Mind, Brain, Wisdom, and instinct knowledge.

they are full filling there object of transformation of peoples Men Women and different creatures of Land water and Sky.

Their vision is very clear influencing the different personates Natures they want Divinity in the infrastructure of whole universe through Spiritualty So every aura of man and every Atom is getting full Divine— Energy through intensity of Receptivity.

Prayer and call have great intension It every one needs transformation.

We only need to surrender our whole being the hype the object or destination, conceding our will and Desire with the Aim of great Rishi's

Words and there objective --- we may make our path of goal of life reality and life's Truth.

At the time influencing the every one's Aura Divine consciousness, may connect with Subjective aura of universal consciousness Aura then every

Soul of this Earth may full fill object of suprema's desire to Heighten the mind at It's spill over object of **Super man**.

Then only this Earth may ignite under the bloom of Sun- Rise of Dream of Supramental consciousness which is the Dream Vision of Lord's contemporary concept of transformation.

10-03-2016 morn 7:30 p.m.

THE MOTHER

Mother is only Authority to- Divert consciousness towards supramental objective confirmation for the universe – considering Now and Then with 4th Dimension.

10-03-2016 morn 07:30 a.m.

FOR THE YEAR 2050

There are so many interfaces of Earth.

But on at 2050 → costume of Divine—Will direct Interfere at vast level to the consciousness and Aura of whole Universe

Then second step Abnormal will start for further Innovation of Mother's Consistency envoy.

19-03-2016 morn 07:00 a.m.

SADHANA

1. Mortality is a phenomena to rusticate adjoined believe system.
2. Since different births we experienced that "Last HR" was totally ignored due to lack of Awareness.
3. There is sequence of interlink of HRS gradually going up to (last) end of HR.
4. Let us revive very Moment of Higher consciousness attending will full desire to achieve the Destination in Real sense of equity when joy and peace is accomplished with Mind, Brain, Wisdom and Soul.
5. Lastly Soul knows whether to Leave Body adjoining all faculties of Doctrines:- where every cell or atom getting Life force Energy to full fill the desire of Supreme.
6. This is journey to supreme then no reason to leave the world till object subjective configuration of "Universal- Truth" is sworn.
7. Hence As per Mother inside applicable strong Desire
8. Savitri adjoined the consciousness of cosmos from that origin --- every heart is getting required energy to decompose the different bad elements of impurities.
9. Then inherit Chaitya Psychic of Mother may reward for transformation and resolve the Death sentenced by ------ then Authority of God.

04-06-2016 morn 05:30 a.m.

YEAR OF 2050 CONTINUED.....

Temptation will Inherit the whole Universe through Divine cosmic energy

there is a vast transforming creativity a few still imparting destination covered synopsis of New Race imprint of Spiritual wave consigned.

This a Historical Era "continuing Further gradation upward Zone-verifying consortium of deity.

All it is magic return of award of "MAA -Bhagwati" what Shri Aurobindo preyed and priest consciousness.

It is a Beating Retreat (convocation on Earth)

15-08-2016 morn 08:00 a.m.

SHRI AUROBINDO

Where there is;-

Words are not uttering, heart is blowing, whole body is in a Static- Trans then there is a thin energy fully flow:

To know thyself your works, to divert whole Humanity towards main objective of your's.

Let the God remind every body to understand Integral- Yoga.

To opt the exact way of Divine.

PRAYER

O Supreme,

Let the visual Intensity works to Individual – Inner consciousness to enlighten the way of- Supramental psychosis adjective so that universe may transform Entire Earth is praying the same.

There is systematic process of Apparel – forces when works then consciousness is widen to approach Ascent/Descent.

15-12-2016 morn 011:00 p.m.

NEW ARRIVAL (OF SOUL)

On prayer of new Arrival of Guest: (I welcomed by heart)

You determine you rationalism.

I will explain my rapture of new world with joy and optimism.

In word the things—in operated playable Role of Discovered New Inventive-- Ideas thoughts and experiences there of and do Theism passion and active role of personality in coming Areas of Present becoming Past and future as a whole being.

16-12-2016 morn. 05:30 a.m.

SHRI AUROBINDO

Five thousand years – has been bestowed by Divine though Shri Aurobindo's Evolutionary- Dream Project Incarnated in forced – creativity.

All though this was Earth's provocation prayed to Supreme at the Threshold of centenary of Shri Aurobindo's Left It was pre decided by shuttle- Physic inward focused though clairvoyance all the weavings has been done for futuristic compose to become Presence of Divine Mother.

12-04-2017 morn. 05:15 a.m.

SAVITRI

Savitri indorsed to all faculties of mind, body, and intellect with super natural powers of spiritualization to work upon- Supreme- consciousness so She replied to all intervenors and other same powers to identify the Truth and sacrifice and to get freedom from all Ancient slavery things of Deadly Instinct.

18-05-2017 morn. 10:00 p.m.

BREADTH

By attaining unavailing wrath of Breathings—you will reach to ocean of un limit.

Try ever best of efforts; How to make 'Silent', breadth (exhale and inhale) where only- soul is in action, there will be in spiritual identity of Divine.

16-06-2017 morn. 07:00 a.m.

SHRI MAA- SHRI AUROBINDO

Beauty of the Divine in the corporeal Body of Shri Aurobindo.

When Mother met first to Shri Aurobindo then with Divine's Legacy: Surrender and Transformation both happened as witness by Earth.

16-06-2017 morn 07:30 p.m.

DEATH

Death: is peculiar Response of the Mother, to Protect the Body, till transformation we should know to give as a whole through prescribed surrender.

Then with full freedom It's Mother to worry for us.

15-07-2017 morn. 05:00 a.m.

SLEEP AND PEACE

Sleep: is the environmental process of Peace.

All the thoughts in encircling in the mind respond for Restless position when they are withheld go behind subconscious, An condition comes when Body, get relaxed slowly- slowly.

We have to aware of kind and type of thoughts coming, going through Nature of Earth.

How we are doing and working upon daily routine work.

Let us know our self:-

Body is some where inconscient we work upon body through Mind, Wisdom, Brain, it acts accordingly, How ever Past is working always upon whole being, it tends to become good- vision, bad-vision finally converted into Joy are tension.

If we want to live in the Present, Forget grief, Depression of the Past come to Present and think How to behave with us, so that life may be joy able at future Past both.

All the competition and contradiction, confusion is within **Us** and no any where.

It depend upon whether come out from un relevant Position or sink.

14-08-2017 a.m. 06:00 a.m.

IGNORANCE

Intercepting the device of Ignorance we are always going towards- Divinity.

One after one crossing the self determination comes through- Inner Voice – this journey is continue since last Era……… and will be continue till last on, connecting with Mother's Evolution submerging with Suprema's Desire, the "Destination" comes through Shri Aurobindo It begins since his Birth……… and will end till Heaven is Sworn.

It's a blazer reward of Shri Aurobindo to this Earth through cosmic reverence and God's Grace.

18-08-2017 morn. 05:15 a.m.

SELF DESIRE OF DEATH

Provocated desire—always works in the direction of will- power.

It's amazing to corelate the desire with different grades of Mind, Vital, Energy, Intellect and get solution as needed.

Since very beginning or different Era and costume of related Time-Sequence Man is lived with very Simple- Mind or Intellect with more exercise of thinking As the Time goes Man become completed according to when he Lived in society City or country.

From the ancient Time, He cared for Food by killing Animals only – After some Time He Attacked on Person.

Since that Time adoration begins Now the Time come that Pressure on Mind, Brain, Vital, Mental, Physical is unanimated increased.

That's why- Suicidal Events terror, dominating Powers, and terror on Self increased – Magically. Drastically, mostly Everybody is on the Target of Provocated thinking and desire and decreased increased like; B.P., tension cancer or other related mental and physical disease.

Environment is Beyond control of Nature due to Man practice of selfish determination than what is solution? God knows only, In fact He has determined to make Free Determination for Each and Every one.

All this Sanskar adjoining in different Era: i.e. – Treat- Yug Dwaper- Yug, Kal- Yug etc.

Doman power is Dominating power some where God interferes by mean of AVTAAR but result was not O.K. as needed.

Know Days occult powers working on every one in different shapes, Superficial Mind thing to be power full Inner Mind Inner- consciousness

Is also not free to determined as per Gods Desire as per God Desires.

Physical World: Mental, Vital World – they full fill there Ego in any direction.

In spiritual world: till the six sense awaken, clairvoyance come the person is working on free desire of Mind set and Sanskar of previous births Chains.

Hence It is difficult to say what kind of desire working in Natural Death, Suicidal Death, Accidental Death, Emanating deficiency of power working in the case of spiritual world also all the Sadhaks must know— the devotion by clairvoyance only

Every category of different system of doctrines is confusing in real sense of adoption of Correct Rout, when Inner voice cultivating Desire of Supreme.

So be very alert and know How to be Body, Mind, Mental, Physical- **Aware** for the **Aim** which you made to get consciousness in every filled of Spiritual- Identity to God.

Shri Maa Shri Aurobindo working on this filled – from Birth to Death and After Death, since beginning of Earth till coming of Supramental Son.

we must know how to abject the desire of individual with Mother's Desire to be conscious from Body to Soul in Crystal Form and filtered up to Hight of Superman Latus pray from the Depth of Inner consciousness that only:-- Mother's Agenda is full filled. In real sense to make this **cosmos** accountable to Supreme only.

27-09-2017 morn 04:30 p.m.

UNTIRING THE ALL AGES OF EARTH INTO RELATIVE SPIRITUAL COSMOS

Why not all the circumstances- come together to become-

Supramental world

This Iconic effort was done evidently by Shri Maa, Shri Aurobindo with the help of Worldly, Mother Here Mother, collected individual destine of every one and work upon the long-long back births and this births to regulate the desires to become "One" for "One" and only Divine this great work will- manipulate the Karm, Gyan, Bhakti, with Identity to Supreme to get only Aim of Subjective Mission of Chatiya- Purush.

Hence open all the doors of whole being so that fresh, pure Air of Receptivity may Transform into one Vision of Shri Maa and Shri Aurobindo that is "HEAVEN" Launch at the Earth forever consecrating all the **Yugs**.

02-10-2017 morn. 07:00 a.m.

BROCHURE OF GRACE

This mission is Reciprocal Project for Divinity empiring on cosmic interphase of Brilliant consciousness. Here is a long path of Humanity for total transformation into Heaven Content Universe, adject to the Vision of Shri Aurobindo's Communion Response of Spirituality approved by Supreme's consign Agreement.

It is not calculated Time- Factor- but visual intensity of Future to be opened to different chapters of great Opportunity give to Earth for "Her" Ancient Prayers now come to the Solution as Reward of Divine.

Meaning of Total Transformation:-

Yes it is Meaning full Preservation of Shuttle- Physic in Higher plane of consciousness for different types of Devotees to exact the Demand of Rational Diversity of Super-man.

2030 will be Touch of Brochure of Grace of Divine.

19-11-2017 a.m. 05:15 a.m.

THE MOTHER

Her Excellency is Governing all the creatures and National Phenomena's of Earth by Variant power--- till Heaven confirm to the Extent of it's Existence super Natural power may not entrust.

The things Happening of Dual Disaster and construction in a Sequence, MOTHER needs it by command of Kali and Maha Saraswati.

The Vision is very clear by Monstrous way, Till it's Shapes by Divine.

It is the true Target of Mother.

Pray: All the callings are adjoin Simultaneously, no one is left.

In this Spiritual Mission and Energy Occult Warriors, because only "Victory" is Waiting, SUN is to Shine and Ignorant- Dark is to invading.

28-11-2017 morn. 05:30 a.m.

DEPARTURE OF MOTHER

(17 NOVEMBER)

Final Destination is achieved by virtue of Divine; Submerged to the mighty Earth's Soul.

Let me confine gratitude to the Supreme.

All of you present this time witness the Sovereignty is Assuring what Regarded by Shri Aurobindo "As" in him- Dream- Vision.

As Mother Allocated................. this Intuited time is always Present in the Past and Future of Gracious Cosmic- Energy of Earth.

28-11-2017 a.m. 07:00 a.m.

TIME

Time is Static and Dynamic- Both.

Let the state of consciousness decide, where is the sequence to upgrade the events and incidents within.

It is environmental Truth that Earth is experiencing his Nature being under disaster.

Let the Man- Conquer the Truth of save the Earth to Live and Love.

Now It's Time to rediscover the Inner conscient to achieve the Target that Divine may convergent the main issue of Man to transform Self and Change the Universe in Dynamic Spirituality which is only solution to See the God in the every cell of Earth.

05-12-2017 morn. 05:00 a.m.

SHRI AUROBINDO'S JOURNEY

On this Eve;

His Perennial journey: is to held an new- cosmos of Divine- Aesthetic- Era, where we people are- Governed by Supreme's constituency, this Earth may conceive Desire of Wordily – Soul, benediction of Superman may- Sworn accordingly.

By the Regard of Deity, you are always entrusting with Evolutionary Transformation till the last **One** is ever breadth unto your governing body.

Prayer:-

O Lord,

We pray for "HIS" New- Convention of Divinity come down to this Earth.

Since His Descent from 15 August to 5 December Ascent Responsive consistency of Earth's Evolution Takes place, As Desire by Supremacy.

27-12-2017 morn 06:00 a.m.

THE MOTHER

Mother has invented the "MAN" in it's cause of Survival in Divine condition "It is surgical operation by Devastating knife" –

She has Located the Every- Moment of every Person for Higher Mountain in Spiritual content visibility.

What **She** has Spoken or drives is the field of derivatives converted into Books- is living – legend for MAN's transformation I.e.;

a. Habits b. Nature c. Behavior d. Sanskars of Births till now-- to make him Superior MAN liable to Supramental Era.

The whole things happening in the field of Environment of whole Universe, whether it is creature of Land, Water, Sky, -- there is a vast informal destruction, combustion which is most necessary because there is Dynamic, Static, Pressure of:-

Maha Sarawati, Maheshwari and finally Mahakali adventing "Heaven" and It is Vision Document of Mother and Shri Aurobindo Precipitated through Supreme's excellency

08-01-2018 morn. 06:30 a.m.

SADHNA

Mandatory This world is not for your's, and you are not for this world.

Think where is equilibrium just see around your self.

You must make this world likely to be live and be adjacent to the world.

It is not see that environment of Universe may not tally with environment of you resulting vice- versa in all respect of outer and inner consciousness of both Elements.

Considering the fact. **Past** was very furious Hence is the **Present** and may be the **Future.**

Volcano is inner disturbance, same is with you so other factors like Wind, Storm and Sea Respectively.

Now days:

It's time to exact the peace within and with worlds........ outer layer of Land as well as inner Integrity.

All disturbances when adjoin to calm then transformation takes place.

Since last few years, Shri Aurobindo is working for the same Project.

Final destination is totally reachable through Shuttle-Physic.

Each and every thing is being processed on Shuttle-Physic for conversion of Hatred, Competition Disaster – into Love all Time.

Only "Love" is master key to open the Door of Heaven.

Let us pry for the reconciliation of Inner Personality of all being of **One an all.**

Will take new birth for whole Land Simple way is only to Pray with Mother till final Reply by her that give peace to me by Love Maa.

20-01-2018 morn 06:00 a.m.

GRACE

In fact: Thy Grace is working and flipping Response earnestly.

Chance is rarest and rare.

Take it as……… what happens when your life consumes Spiritual Identity according to knowledge and instinct.

No if, and but go straight and round.

There is an- empathy surrounding. Your whole being.

Still:

You have to come out you're your creation Illusion, Delusion…. and hurts.

What is necessary will be your—Destination and destiny.

Outward – things may be Left, Insight to Grow and accept as it is.

"Time" is bestowed catch the moment of concern.

01-02-2018 morn 06:00 a.m.

GRATITUDE

Hence we are under taking the pledge of Gratitude.

Will in hence – power of Grace where we start with Spirituality step by step.

Gratitude: is invariably, Surrender with counter part of "EGO" earnestly not required.

Deeply we are seeing the 'Things as it is' – and awareness of each moment what to do and not to do.

How the Mother's Desire enveloping the whole being it is time to Perceive………… And increase the receptivity with Internal "Integral Yoga".

02-03-2018 morn. 04:00 a.m.

THE MOTHER

There is a celestial touch of "Mother" to every Atom of Universe – being transformed.

Every where is extension of Divine Love Speedup Rapidly.

Overlapping all disintegrated ugly things: eg, **दुश्मनी ईर्षा, व्देष कामना वैमनस्य हिंसा, वासना, स्पर्धा.**

श्री अरविन्द की "DREAM -VISION" **का मतलब:**

सूक्ष्म भौतिक जगत का शस्वत परिदृय वर्तमान को वर्धमान कर रहा है

तब तक

जब तक

सूर्यालोकित न हो जाये।

05-02-2018 morn. 05:00 a.m.

SADHNA

You have come from there and to go there.

In between the things are- alleged.

Be clear about your Self other self and transducer. Testimony is different. Be receptive by virtue of regard then-

You get things as it is.

Whole things are conferral and Hide.

21-03-2018 morn. 05:00 a.m.

JOURNEY UN LIMIT

Don't say 'NO' to the Last.

Try to know and understand say to subconscious to be conscious for the Last.

It is long way of subconscious then it will reach to conscious.

Although Last breadth is not some where fixed but it is prolonged in respect to Harassment, fear and insecurity,

It is journey from Awaken mind to Awaken Soul Hence it is journey of un limit.

Here are some points:-

Register the Death and count the velocity-

a. Every HR is precious.
b. Every moment is in between Agree/ Disagree.

For that very type of consciousness

Let us experience and sit silently and see before whether to Heighten or Lower the consciousness when Time comes.

Preparation is important because Mother is: experiencing with each -soul with future stick and Present involvement to get ready for, transformation.

Every Sadhak has Dream- Vision with eyes of Mother.

You have to realize the same with deep consensus and Heart desire.

Let us breadth with the breadth of Mother.

Reach to the conclusion and cross the Illusion by this prayer:-

O Beloved Mother.

Let the "Love" and "Bliss" come through your consciousness to envelop all Disintegration and clear the exact way of your's.

11-10-2018 morn. 08:15 a.m.

STAGE OF UPPER STANDARD CONSCIOUSNESS

Tranquilization and radicalization of whole – mind and Body System by - imperial- PEACE was preserved earlier now things are-- happening as per Mother's concealed Desire.

Here Follow every turn of Moment and consciousness is upgrading accordingly, Be Alert of desperated occult forces, Let it pass away.

Hence ardent PEACE is within Heart and every cell Responding.

29-10-2018 morn. 06:30 a.m.

PEACE

Utmost peace—

Cultivate the whole system of: Mind, Body, wisdom, Intelligence ignorance, Knowledge towards Improvement.

Insisting upon Desire- Consistency old myths and Past affirmations we must Know to come out of Barriers of Sanskar's of Back Births.

Must know of Governing Bodies. Who carry the Present Stop and see the Self of existence every Hour working under mis concept.

Every Cell of Body responding the same, conversing into Pressure of Blood tension, Aggravations, depressions, Etc.

Around as –

The Persons are open books to study every page and Download the system of Improvement into Peace full Mind.

Be judgmental on every Action and Reaction to our nearest, dearest with eye of empathy

We must know our contribution towards Humanity and there Sorrow and Joy in Real Sense.

21-10-2018 morn 05:00 a.m.

LOVE

Whimsical Mistake- Should not be, where love disqualifies the Parental Truth.

Love —

1. Which surrounds with Hatred conceived stream of believe system— due to selfish Fina mina.
2. Man is alone of get not receptive sense, where he find's Empathy.
3. Whole environment of Universe Including SKY Lark is Full of Attraction and Esteem Love How ever Man is kept apart now days.

So all the vibrations Emotions feelings, is under the coverage of Loneliness and so Mind is under coverage of Tense and depression every where.

He does not wants to understand "things as it is"—

Always Subconscious mind is full of Disintegration and divided, not United and Disciplined.

11-10-2018 morn 04:45 a.m.

COLLECTIVE MEDITATION

In collective meditation—one has to be very alert and Important is 'Rejuvenation' of Individual.

Wordily Soul is determined by Mother:- to interconnect every Soul towards Higher Object.

In this Regard Let us See;

Every step towards Higher consciousness is beginning to every mount but accountability: is first step towards Mother's Desire.

To cope with Love, Sincerity, Honesty—towards Destination what Mother says is only '**Supreme**' Apart leaving all Desires of individual and any Other(as group).

To Forget Past and live in Present is main criteria of Sadhna.

First way—

Allegation will not work but alleviation to wards "Individual Development" may be priority if told to any other person.

17-11-2018 morn 05:00 a.m.

INERT EDUCATION

Inert Education – is must for every Body, nowadays.

What we see outward is not true some time.

Bhagwat Gita is reference Book for this purpose.

We always live in two Parts:-

One is mind

Second is wisdom

Third one is encyclopedia: i.e.

Sixth Sense,

What we choose we live that,

Six sense: first come like a flickering Light till it's device Light-up.

Most of the compassions are cause of old and New birth.

We have to separate Our Self from Self.

Witness the whole incoming and outgoing by brilliant surrender of whole being to the God – Head of warrior.

11-12-2018 morn 06:00 a.m.

INERT EDUCATION

Inert Education – is must for every Body, nowadays.

What we see outward is not true some time.

Bhagwat Gita is reference Book for this purpose.

We always live in two Parts:-

One is mind

Second is wisdom

Third one is encyclopedia: i.e.

Sixth Sense,

What we choose we live that,

Six sense: first come like a flickering Light till it's device Light-up.

Most of the compassions are cause of old and New birth.

We have to separate Our Self from Self.

Witness the whole incoming and out going by brilliant surrender of whole being to the God – Head of warrior.

Mother's consistency

You are a part of great – Revolution which under ways (acknowledge) with—

Mother's

Conservative-

Transformation

Grace is always in- right Direction always not will full to you.

Hence be receptive towards God-- Head Inspirations.

02-01-2019 morn 06:30 a.m.

YUGA'S CONCESSIONS

After constitution of "Four- YUGS"- with Collaboration of Divine, Lord— Reveled next destination of Supramental Instinct Observatory- Cell.

By Dismantling All deformations of Then, mounting DIVINE- TRUTH over All falsehood.

This Pyramid will safe and secure all the five- Elements, 14 Loks (**14 लोक**) of Devta's Constructive Cell.

This Lattice Movement is continue since opening Door and Golden Wave Brought down to the Earth.

Resting over Subjective—Truth—MAN is the main target, all the concealment is gradually opening by structing old Myths, believes, Thought pattern at subconscious and conscious enveloped Demon- Forces till the- man is Ready.

It's will take time up to limit then – **Time** will drive-

All consequences and circumstances through Mother's excellency by It's own objective Mission.

Every thing was prepared in Shuttle – Physic by expert and Reverential outfit.

Mother is now not asking for readiness (now days) but She Superseded your all the Desire and Demands in Preparation of your self.

One man Agenda is:-

If you are Ready or not, Time is over.

May Earnest Desire with will full compliment of Shri Aurobindo consigning Determination of Spiritual Divine World of Golden Race is Ready to confine Supramental Body into **"जड चेतना में आविर्भाव होगी प्रभु सर्जित चेतना समस्त अंधकार प्रकाति होंगे एक दिव्य अहंभाव द्वारा नवागंतुक–युग में"।**

Mania determination of Mother will superb—all the determinations and desires finally will construct Divine compulsion Resolution ERA.

03-01-2019 morn 08:00 a.m.

INTROVERT

delicate Introvert Subconscious is coming out – be aware of Entire corrigendum.

Endurance of Regard will come up within ------ Time Sequence.

By omitting the Past clearing the Future let the Present Illumine the Peace, Subconscious may be established in New ERA.

Look; that every thought is the Working Pattern of your Life Hence consciousness is the Main Factor.

Cognitive Award is given by Imperative Power you have to understand by Inner consensus.

18-02-2019 morn 07:00 a.m.

THE MOTHER

The mother is Selected 'Soul' of Divergent **Supreme** ever come on the Earth—by Call of Spiritual Powers Dominating Demon Forces, Finally to Bring Kingdom of God.

Accountability and Responsibility to the Individual Soul will bring-near to Her Divine project.

"Time" -- wishes you circumstances may follow the Real Devotee of upcoming Heaven.

21-02-2019 morn 06:00 a.m.

DARSHAN-DAY

Full focus on- Divine Created Time (Including- Past, future, and Present) where and – what Mother has accommodated you and every devotee you must aware by Generated Awaken consciousness Inner outer Spiritual Environment has been- Changed.

Full surrender is first priority by acknowledging intuitive certify, modify Instinct, every where is Presence of Mother must be experienced by—clairvoyance.

Then you will work what 'She' Desire.

26-02-2019 eve 11:25 p.m.

THE MOTHER

With the Divine trust --- Mother plunges you from the Past.

And bring you to the Real Plate form of Present from where you way uplifted by Inner consciousness; (Soul)

27-02-2019 morn 6:00 a.m.

PLEASE

Don't please.

your self.

Or other self

Please the Lord.

Then you will be

In Harmony with

World-self.

27-02-2019 night 11:00 p.m.

TANTRA

Tantra:-

Is the total believe system, on how to condemn self and other where Naked-Soul, installed on body consciousness in fused the whole layers of mind, Brain, finally it is game of………. Subjected and materialistic world how to attract Demonic forces – from clutch of Impaired Holistic Approach of spiritual contentment.

03-03-2019 morn 06:00 a.m.

SADHNA

Past :

Govern me, so is the future simultaneously.

Past means :-

Back birth, bigger Past – is most suspicious- decides most of activities each and every Breadths: decides – Departure gradually.

Breadth system, thought pattern is controlled by most of the aggressions provocations, inspite peace and calm- where is the Present only past-ingredient.

search carefully only by Mother's attitude and Desire of Divine only solution is;

Liberate from the Past by well- Being and Emerge **it** to the Mother's resolution; (total surrender)

31-03-2019 morn 05:00am

MOTHER

Majestic time is quite managed by holy consciousness through Mother.

Hence no question of devotee concern, a part of the effort let the Mother think, do, be for your bigger self and inner outer orbit of your existence.

But even you are not ready due to past reconciled future converted in to present and this is being happened since so many traditional cultures of back births.

Then when circumstances are accommodated by divinity then you will find your exact place, where you will Ready as Mother always inspire you.

She the beauty how mother trapped attribute, aesthetic sense inclined with stint power and knowledge towards one-ness. When surrender is only an only advent.

Man can get relax spiritually when opposite poles of his nurtured nature are adjoined in to One.

Mother does the same sometimes, She catches your past, present, future then combines till the awaken of consciousness hence submit your all the mathematical impression, Calculation of your mind and wisdom everyday let, Her aggregate your contribution and decide accordingly.

Then you will see what the mother wants finally- all the possibility are hidden behind. Your applications of diversity towards true-Self.

02-04-2019 morn 05:15 am

YEAR- 2050 (YEAR OF COMPASSION)

Year of compassion is compressed in inferno of revised time slot.

Person concern will experience with determined will of ecstasy with and speculation and Divine Mother is extensive era of Supramental enhancement coverage on wide range of Universe.

Hence 2050 will by cherished year of the Mother.

"Thy" will always look forward and look after your will must conceive if even in all difficulties and tolerances with consigned efficacy.

Person concern (means): departed soul and on way to departure with Mother's consistency imprisoned revolutionary vision.

02-04-2019 morn 06:00 am

SAVITRI

Although in response of the developed divine conciseness "Savitri" is defined or redefined.

But One must know togetherness of inspirations by deity, explanations are depicted in deferent forms of reconciled integrated inner awaken consensus.

However all Mantras are upgraded stairs of spiritual mounts, you should be perceiver by your own prayer, that how long is your sunlit path and what is your destination in true-sense only Mother can know.

Hence your eyes. Hands. Legs. Mind. Intellect and full body components and all channels of inner conciseness (include soul) must be reckoned by Mother only.

04-04-2019 morn 07:45 am

ON 11TH JANUARY 2014 MOTHER'S PRAYERS AND MEDITATION

All the complications has been bestowed due to circumstantial apprehension it is the past extension impowered how sell Mother has innovative contrived transformation has been promised by God's awareness, But the people not capable to get immerging total diversity will change all unchangeable, then love and beauty will superb by victory.

Hence your immortal love is magically massive controller upon earth.

22-08-2019 morn 12:00 am

Let the Mother may enhance
My desire to aware of departure
With instinct Knowledge.

So as to reach:-

Destination which Mother knows
And desire for upgradation towards
Transforming object of notion of being.

05-04-2019 night. 10:00 p.m.

THE MOTHER

Mother: Has redefined prospects of "in scripted" knowledge of till now. How She dared to cross the limitation of all ways where danger was prescribed whether. It is Disease, tension, Aggravation depression education – mental vital emotional or spiritual- etc.

Finally, she made approach road from heart to soul then supreme to identify the surrender by Egoism itself till the true-self sworn.

Now all type of conventional form of intensify and awaken souls has been put-up to the one platform of Mother's celestial- touch –

They are intending to go forward on the sun -lit path each and every struggle effort difficulty of present and back births is being resolved to mount the object by- subjective resources where the whole mission is under dream vision of Shri Aurobindo

Will take leap by **year 2050** and clear vision of supramental world will take shape of Mother's desire of Auroville in each Heart and each soul of cosmic Rhythm.

Hence: It is all – manifestation of truth under the Guidance of Divine Mother.

Truth:

Ambient truth which aggregate All the – Energy formations intoxicated by Inner outer calibrations from meta physical as well as. Materialistic world integrated into O**ne Ness**

06.04.2019 morn. 05.00 a.m.

SADHNA

Majestic time, is quite managed by holy consciousness through mother

Hence is no question of devotee concern – apart of efforts let the mother think do see for your bigger self and inner outer orbit of your existence

But even you are not ready due to past reconciled future converted into present, and this is being happened since so many traditional cultures of back births.

Then when circumstances are accommodated by Divinity then you will find your exact place, where you will ready as mother always inspire you. See the beauty ... now mother trapped attribute aesthetic sense inclined with instinct, power and knowledge towards **one-ness** – when surrender is only and only advent.

Man can get relax spiritually when opposite poles of his nurtured nature are adjoined into **one**. Mother does the same sometimes, she catches your past, Present, Future then combines till the awaken the consciousness.

Hence submit your all the mathematical impression calculation of your mind and wisdom – everyday let See aggregate your contribution and decide accordingly.

Then you will see – what the mother wants finally – all the possibilities are hidden behind your applications of diversity towards true self.

07.04.2019 morn. 06:00 a.m.

SELECTION AT A GLANCE

Always – we follow multitude selection with our superficial mind and intellect because we are for runner of past births. There are four categories :--

1. Mindset to visualize objective of materialistic world.
2. To visualize objective of new redefined world.
3. To visualize objective of spiritual subjective intense by gradually upgraded consciousness.
4. To visualize objective to receive exact aim with follow – god's measurement till the Grace works fully by instinct.

   Most of the time three categories drives us:--

   1. Sattvic
   2. Rajsic
   3. Tamsic

Prestigious form of mixed categories less of more works by invaded nature simultaneously till final destination come up. **Ignorant** is gradually increased or decreased into contaminated farm of Six Sense.—where we find glimpses of light We run very fast , without differentiate Moon or Sun diligently, we should know observant of consciousness with determination with peace.

Follow the path of.. who can give you first step to climb the mountain without fear, contradiction are conflict

Here you must elect the "one" Guru, Sadguru or Master with fully devotion without applicable Ego.. etc.

To connect Oneness of all faculties inner or outer being.

You sit with prayer and total silence – selection and rejection will be automatically according to Grace found, then will be your exact Destination.

Everywhere – Thumb rule of attraction is not applied, because there are gravitational forces, beneath and above the Earth.

There is only Centrifugal force—is once applicable will work up to fourth Dimension

08-04-2019 morn. 06:00 a.m.

SHAVITRI

Although – in response of the developed Divine consciousness "Shavitri" is defined or redefined, but one must know: togetherness of Inspirations by Deity Explanations are depicted in different forms of Reconciled Integrated inner Awaken consensus.

How ever All Mantras are upgraded Stairs of Spiritual Mounts, you should by perceiver by your own prayor , that how long is your Sunlit - Path, and what is your destination in true sense only Mother can know, Hence—

Your Eyes, Hands, lags Mind, Intellect, and full body components and all channels of Inner consciousness must be (Including Soul) reckoned by Mother only.

16.05.2019 night. 09.15 p.m.

THE MOTHER

"Mother"—is engraving, investing, initiating your life's and Births, till the transformation this multitasking dynamic work only "SHE" is doing, managing ever done in the History of universe and Whole Earth.

It's quite Amazing

22-05-2019 morn. 06:30 a.m.

SADHNA

Every Past and Future is controlled by Present and that is omni-Presence.

We can witness the **same** by empowering True-Self, than Things may be placed on It's original State, provided consciousness is awaken.

31.05.2019 morn. 06.40 a.m.

THE MOTHER

I have to await for the Mother's decision.

Mother:-

Decides after long period when you do not decide. She interferes in each moment of your life.

Hence Equation of Surrender begins when and till the whole being – Submerge into Mother's Will and Desire.

What the Mother's Specific Agenda is to Prepare: this – Earth for consideration of Dream Vision of Divine Consigning Shuttle—Physic, of 4th Dimensional view of Supreme Desire, Through Shri Aurobindo's unconditional Spiritual Identifications ever seen till the all four Yug – emerge into Heaven's Supramental Era.

21-06-2019 morn. 05:10 a.m.

DEATH

Death:-

Is Divided into four prominent -Figures,

A- Leaving of mind
B- Leaving of Intellect
C- Leaving of PRAN
D- Leaving of Soul

It is distinct course ever Inspired by Different Sadgurus or Directives, then It depends upon which **One** is principal creative -force upon you.

Whole thing is "Spiritual field" enforced.

You have come to this Earth or sent for specific – purpose, which is known, or unknown or major mystic formulas due to ignorance.

"HE" knows that you have forgotten the things due to collective energies may be Dark or Light Depends upon- Karmic Evidences, entire Back Births.

Now you adject the Desire if aware of Inner consciousness process is long or prolonged.

Your life Style must be adjacent to spiritual Identities, when Real Advent life begins – with Sadguru, then every moment is developed by soul-consciousness.

then it should drive your-

A- Mind
B- Intellect
C- Pran
D- And other faculty of your being till the Real Aim is focused by own "Chaitya" impowering all—Adjective Administers, Incorporeal things
E- Then all above is contorted by Beloved Mother.
F- Here you are under the guidance of Mother's Agendas, To reach the objective of supramental.

G- New Innovative Govern consigned by Shri Aurobindo at- Psychic level of Divine and suprema's realistic Heaven.

H- Hence you should not ready for Death till Mother insist for your Desire to await preparation for new births. By Clairvoyance which only Mother knows. And you can only pray to Mother for her Grace and Blessing which Hides, your Life's objective and determination to leave the body.

22-06-2019 morn. 06:30 a.m.

THE MOTHER

Mother:-

Has spread over all the Energy Fields of Divine to the Earth or Whole Universe.

So you Feel the same at your level as it was at the level of Pondicherry Ashram at all celebration Days due to impartial comprehensive – Electro magnetic fields and spiritual waves or wave lengths all you are breathings under her life supporting's whole system of nature Environment of Earth.

Her platform is ready to reach her secret Agenda if you are ready to wipe whole Past.

Be affirmative of your desires finished except diversion of whole being increasing receptivity towards her Desire, Grace, and Blessings then Mother will—see for your best.

"She" – may impower your witness to see the things if required for you – provide surrender takes place Gradually and Rationally.

23.06.2019 morn. 05.30 a.m.

SHRI AUROBINDO SOCIETY CENTER'S CONFIRMATION

All the centers:-

Must be developed by it's own strategy.

Your wish list is prolonged due to unapproachable unwanted desires, whether they are any type of Administrations, but Analyze the Past, She the present exceed the panorama of Structure in the Direction of:---

a- What is the main factor who can visualize the every member in the mirror of spiritual Identity with the core of Heart.

b- See that our wish list should not widen and long --- with respect to mind, Intellect, finally Soul- consciousness is important.

c- only advent procedure of prayer may bring the real development provided feedback is seen from time to time. But collective prayer who is works must be perceived.

d- Don't leave on Mother any thing until you know: How instinct works at full swing.

e- Mother always see:--

Un Fathomless favors how real devotee brings His consciousness to see the desire (deep desire) to be connected with each word, spoken and written by her own spirit – empowered to conform consciousness and transfer into the real destination of Supramental Era which is not so simple.

09-07-2019 morn. 05:30 a.m.

BODY

Physical /Astral **Body** must be perceived- carefully.

Why?

Because it gives – proper knowledge for come to this Earth and acknowledge the period of God's will each and every cell carry the Past and Present and desire to live for some purpose- further make Efforts and Destiny.

When we take each breadth—It brings Hygiene and Disease both according to peace and Aggravation resulting increase and decrease consciousness.

We must learn to live according to mind, and Intellect when they are Approaching in the right and positive Direction with regard to inner or outer consciousness.

What is Premium Truth of the Life's opportunity; God's desire and It's acknowledgement at the Depth.

27-07-2019 morn. 06:00 a.m.

SYNTHESIS OF YOGA

All the Avoidable things are—

Left behind as per response of adequate Light and Energy.

Here it is extensive achievement of Divine so the Transformation Commences gradually by devotion and Ego manifestation till the grace is completely see the Suprema's desire a innovative truth.

21-07-2019 morn. 05:10 a.m

ASCENT-DESCENT

More then- authenticity and knowledge is required for whole being; Body, Mind, and other faculties of Inner outer Orbit, "Grace" will do what ever it is needed for your Goodness and wellness, Provided what ever you pray by inner consciousness in response of dedication gradually increasing by calling Mother's Light, Energy with deep Desire and consensus.

Further Accent- Descent is regular ally commences as consciousness is Brighter and Wider.

In this whole process our Intelligence and cleverness will not work except of Humanity and Gratitude shown towards Mother, Lord every moment.

At that Day when you understand “HIS” cleverness completely --- then you need not to do anything then **HE** will govern.

As prakriti, Purush adjoin you at all levels of mountains.

02-08-2019 morn. 05:15 a.m.

DESTINY

Reversal of Destiny --- is prone to proper prayer by Soul.

It is Indigenous matter connected with Nature and it’s Lord.

Here all the working patterns are reconciled by covert promising objects of Individuals.

It is deep concern – with shuttle physic and approach.

Only Grace can Advocate and Interrogation takes place accordingly.

Some where responsive births, are to be determined by different Visions of Inner consciousness and Past meridians, clairvoyance plays important Roll in this respect.

Finally out SadGuru or Lord has the power to come forward for resolution of the different discrepancies of Self or True -Self.

Beware of the T**hings** that If **HE-** will bring you out of All the crisis.

11-08-2019 morn. 07:00 a.m.

GRACE

Grace is associated with whole Universe and Being.

It invoke and obscure all the difficulties and circumstances.

Finally it will carry you to the destination subjected to Higher consciousness with Divine comprehension.

11-08-2019 morn. 02:00 p.m.

SILENCE

When Silence is totally reciprocate;

Imperial Truth:-

Is there where Supreme Commends whole nature through Pare-Prakriti.

14-08-2019 morn. 07:15 a.m.

SHRI AUROBINDO'S BIRTHDAY

15TH AUGUST

Every Birthday of Shri Aurobindo is the Birthday of Universe and India like wise for the upcoming New Era.

It is all necessary including all events incidents adjoining with Divine compensatory desire.

See that Supreme: adoration decisions of shuttle Physic are quite mark of Humanity to be transform in a single Dream vision ever seen by Prakriti Through Param Chetna.

His Birthday is the Peculiar- day of the India so as to reach Destination of superb Destiny of Earth every prayed by Herself and Her Citizens.

22-08-2019 night 12:00 p.m.

MOTHER

Let the Mother may enhance my Desire to aware of departure with instinct knowledge.

so as to reach destination which Mother knows and desire for upgradation towards transforming object of notion of being.

24-08-2019 morn 05:30 a.m.

PRESENT

If – Present is power full allocation then Past—discriminated automatically after sorted Good/bad selection, rejection.

Some how this moment—should be hold to exact your consciousness towards Higher projections, don't see Hidden behind truth or falsehood events or thoughts committed throughout HRS.

31-08-2019 morn. 06:00 a.m.

SHRI AUROBINDO

He is opened mind

At the highest omnipotent state

For this earth:-

To determine the excellent

Transformation of every creature:-

To be ready first Then to opt the

Way of superseding

All the faculties of

Elements finally reach to the Supramental-Sky of Devine conversant

Blooms regard-

Ever seen by his dream-vision at shuttle physic

of TIME & IMMORTAL will

25-10-2019 morn. 06:15 a.m.

SADHNA WITHIN

In fact – we should tide our honesty towards Sadhna with full concentration- and interference should be taken very diligently.

Every time we should think of 'Lord' by passive and required active mode.

No body should be allowed- the things which downward the consciousness by any how; thought, Believe system, wrong interpretation of impressions of any people of family are outside obstructing the way you opt.

You should adjudge your self are your shadguru from time to time your object must be – to identify the purpose to come to this Earth only.

We Should know:

That what and why we should know, and what not also in the same way, with whom we should ask

Means: all the questions must come on surface and resolved to the inner/ outer orbit of consciousness.

Then the way will we very clear in the Sprint- Light and Darkness will we removed likewise.

Nothing is obligation except of Grace—who drive's your path towards "LIGHT" since birth's Spiritual Ingredients.

31-10-2019 morn. 05:45 a.m.

CONCLUDING PART

Your Life's concluding Part is ---

Breathless – Calm towards Supreme,

Will further decide your next – step for Spiritual Heights and journey of Spirit configuration of—God's Desire for Best of Earth of Golden Future ever Prayed by greater Saints……..i.e.;…… Shri Aurobindo's truth full efforts and Mother's considerations there of.

10-02-2020 morn. 12:00 a.m.

SHRI AUROBINDO

Years 2050--78 will be Great Universal Divine Incident (at world) on the Earth of upcoming Era.

Where Supremacy will witness → transformation of Advent Spiritual world.

It is cognitive and Reverential Recognition of Supreme.

नोट

(उस वक्त श्री अरविन्द, श्री मॉ के सूक्ष्म जगत में पूर्ण प्रकति एवं प्रवेष के सौ वर्ष पूर्ण हो चुके होंगे।)

15-08-2020 06:00 am

SHRI AUROBINDO'S

BIRTH IMPRESSIONS

Conventional, occasional, fillings of this day-

Is exceptional devotional and marginal to the slavery interpretation however it was invented under guidance of supreme. To collaborate with avatar shri Aurobindo to bring quite freedom from all types of distress, troubles, difficulties in the way of spiritual abundance-

Mother has prayed through Earth and cosmic Reverence to bring Humanity at its best form, of ever done in the different coming, going YUG.

however, this was the pattern to consider to open the all Closings till final destination of imprisonment, becomes all the doors of slavery-

Opens towards Dawn.

We are very lucky to see the transformation in all respect by bringing our births. Through Mothers Consignment on Promise by supreme.

That thing has been happened, as was to happened.

When supramental enveloped the whole kingdom of falsehood by advent truth of supreme light of "sun" only.

We all Conventional devotees now breath in the Enlightened path shown by dream vision, of Shri Aurobindo.

SHE Again will witness,

When Shri Aurobindo again come to highlight the efficacy of real freedom for divinity and unite, All souls. Sworn in a lightened body where mind intellect, Pran and ego Transform into Love and Bless of God.

Shri Aurobindo is always present in different farms.

In this universe, till the manifestation of divine.

12-11-2020 morn. 05:00 a.m.

RELICS (INTERVENTION)

Always:

. be humble.

. smile with credibility.

. righteousness may be understood.

. always follow our nescience with honestly and accountability.

. Discover yourself when you are in silence of optimum- inner outer voices of integration.

. Your Receptive mode must be when all type of – meditation grow up with pure relationship of inner soul with surrender.

. when we live with the peace we live with the supreme. Provided grace envelope. With supernal universal and cosmic rhythm soul.

. Here are vibrations of divine convulsion throw out the earth.

. every spot is filled up with mother's interior desire.

. you must know how to invest your energy power and work Manship towards final destination who conceived mother always.

. hence always pray:

Mother

I love you

Which will proceed me towards delight full apprehension and blessing of your's.

whole being is following your determination and commitment.

20-11-2020 morn. 02:00 a.m.

THIS MISSION

See the beauty of the follower like true dream blows, as and when mother has consented:

You should not worry for this birth. Till the total being confirmed for Integral yoga.

This birth or prolonged birth is commune with divine will be delightful and full of blessing and grace.

Then this: mission or project will tally with the final destination of Dream-Vision of shri- Aurobindo as supramental word apprehend exist.

20-11-2020 morn. 02:30 a.m.

MOTHER & HER CHILD

With perspective of divine live how mother is aware with the soul of her son.

There is very reason of true connection with child. It depends upon the progressive consciousness with respect to Her regard and reward by Universal mother.

22-11-2020 morn. 06:00 a.m.

UNITED WORK OF SPIRITUALITY

When we united disguise for the brilliant path of future-------

Which may realize and leads towards Divine- excellency.

Hence when we two or more meet by apparently or without-

Here is opportunity by god to uplift consciousness tends to discover new path and self

Any step towards unanimity has is on impotence towards field of dense spirituality and acknowledge the knowledge karm and instinct.

It is further connectivity towards universal Soul.

That is why collective meditation and prayers further works as which is ultimate aim of the dream vision of Supreme to bring down Heaven upon Earth.

23-11-2020 morn. 03:50 a.m.

GRACE

. We have to prove ourself-

For the "Grace of the Lord"

Always dark prays for the right- till real approach work for the bridge of determination.

. There is space between life ad the death and is expanding only sadguru knows to make every moment opportunity for delightful surrender as it reaches to knowledge of true- self then difficulty turn to the progressive path.

. Relationship is only one- aspiration between intuition and instinct.

24-11-2020 morn. 05:15 a.m.

WILL OF THE SUPREME

Every where is signatured will of the Supreme against your merely desires.

Find it very diligently although it is hidden behind subjective knowledge of consistency.

Open it by eternal constitution of consciousness when united and "one".

25-11-2020 morn. 05:00 a.m.

SIDDHI DAY

Borrower of this secret day is always present.

To dignify the true-self of every people till coming the supramental Age.

All the levels of mind- here are receptive with Supreme.

This time call- will carry the destiny of people to be Divine.

Here we should pray:-

O Divine mother

Let all the souls follow the path of Sun lit path by whole being with existence of self destination adjoining Maharshi Shri Aurobindo's final benediction.

01-12-2020 morn. 05:15 a.m.

SAVITRI

Savitri- saw victory against power of impotent egoism established.

Hence confirms- Immortality power of Regime on earth as per apprised Supreme.

Here opened door of all the resources of spirituality to approve superlative Humanity and It's core for manifestation of Divinity as opportunity given by Golden Age. Ever.

04-11-2020 morn. 06:00 a.m.

SUN-SEERS

We are elected Sun-seers.

Mother has given us Divine convulsion Prospects.

So don't worry of this Birth Earth will witness Supramental coverage……. Inert very shortly wait is no long now.

Unanimity and one ness is very near. Compressed air of Divine consciousness is flowing throughout the universe.

Determined "Time" was already fixed in the space as per Dream Vision of Shri Aurobindo, corresponding to Shuttle Physic.

05-12-2020 morn. 05:30 a.m.

SHRI AUROBINDO'S TRUE-SELF

It's the day when tenebrous world is ready to transform It's best Farm.

Determination of supreme- may invent new Innovative steps towards super consciousness.

Humanity is crowned for golden opportunity. Insist for vigyan-Enlightened future.

HE is present after departure and before.

All the soul's are witnessing: Sunlit path is cultivating new Era It's beginning now up to the Last one.

"It was the Time when HE is ready to awaken all the soul's to ready for this mission".

05-12-2020 morn. 08:45 a.m.

SAVITRI

Endurance of this great Divine- Poetry (Mantr-kavya).

Must be brought inside- and let it grow up to mark without any expectation and prospects.

09-12-2020 morn. 10:50 p.m.

THE MOTHER

The Mother-

She is still enhancing the people sadhak for greater knowledge of Divine and Transformation as per Receptivity.

He who think of Mother by heart "She" is present always.

You can listen her will and vibration may link up with your soul contributing your Awakening towards Sun Lit Path.

Always Remember that blessing and grace will Shower if Trusted and Revealing on HER- vision of distinct way of Supramental world.

12-12-2020 morn. 05:30 a.m.

DAWN

This is Dawn:

Is here adoration of light in the Inertness It is determination of mind- at the highest Level.

When glimpses of Lord is seen apart deities of different Levels An century may convert into HR.

When- seed of Immortality is sowed- and whole Humanity it's Divine farm.

It's an Informal- way of situation that after ascent and descent for a long period of straggle within soul and outer coverage of different forces of Demon consideration finally- promising object of Divine love got victory on- that death which is precipitate of traditional grief sorrow and acknowledgement of yamraj's that site which is ultimate falsehood upon true-self which is Clear cut- aspiration who wants to take all freedoms from Humanity by this kind of death.

Savitri is the formidable light of that Sun which include desire of supreme to Implement Law of Supramental convention to bring down Regime of Lord at every cell and soul of every people by developing psychic and Transformation of whole being of heaven is the Dream Vision of Shri Aurobindo and concealment of Divine Mother.

17-12-2020 morn. 06:00 a.m.

PURIFICATION

Every day is the marvelous day of the excellent Divine,

See, where you stand target must be selected so as to reach at greater mountain then go ahead till your final destination achieved those who created visual intensity towards **Purification** of mind Intellect pran and body you must watch and wait do necessary-

Who carry you towards inside and outside world. Your are Interests must be diminished and emerged into one aspiration of the Governing body of the Divine Mother.

Then only you may Forward ahead step by step. Your mind's creation is parallel to your main object, where policy maker of ego may – Invest your energy to get your personal Achievement of so called personality who believe in Ambition.

Leave apart all the bindings of vital Energy. Liberate from all type of…… thinks may furious you in the materialistic world this is the final world of nothingness among all the Humanity and determination of your self- then only true-self appears.

Which may bring your real approach towards Sun Lit Path.

Only and only one ness with the matured aesthetics of Divinity it is subjected consignment with the surrender to main stream of…… resource of "ONE".

Your have to know to see this great opportunity given by great Mother

20-12-2020 morn. 07:45 a.m.

PEACE

When you pray-

For the peace of universe.

Then it is more and more fruitful.

Then what you require peace for your self.

Hence It is embedded Peace, coming to you through Universe, loyal to Supreme.

30-12-2020 morn. 05:40 a.m.

SHRI AUROBINDO

Crown- of Imperishable- Truth is Always illumined to show the Path of greater truth for- Followers, Devotees and common people respectively immensely.

Corridor is already provided Buildup from Earth to Heaven of promise.

31-12-2020 morn. 05:25 a.m.

MOTHER

Hostile Forces- are working at their earnest level.

What is responsive factor of this Govern privilege.

Not HE is but you will be known After ward.

Always Mother is unprecedented regard at every moment is precious for your consciousness getting upward.

06-01-2021 morn. 04:20 p.m.

WAR OF REVENGE

Sabotage Energy-

To be utilized very confidently and conveniently Preliminary test is done.

Independent forces- are mediatory devices to stop the destruction.

All the countries are governed by prestigious demitasse ill-will dark Energies.

We should always now thank full to GOD- for "insight Vision" and- peace full projection of mission who is under taken by spiritual Diversion of universe towards Pleasant Divine.

So gratitude for the same and pray for new Era Commencing through Dream vision of Shri Aurobindo.

All are determined facts: After great work effort inspired by Supreme.

06-01-2021 morn. 07:00 a.m.

THE MOTHER

It's perpetual Art of living.

To be with the Mother throughout the HRS.

Time slot to be divided into undivided consciousness while working thinking doing every work.

But remember and surrender each and every thing. Will carry you towards transformation through psychic being.

Your every object must be very clear.

Why you are here and how brought-up.

To which you belong and who are you? Always-

Within mind- intellect and finally with soul.

It's spiritual journey to envisage your self for a part of determination with peace for certain object fixed by Mother Intensify your whole being towards SUN LIT PATH going towards new Era of supramental world's pre decided.

23-02-2021 morn. 10:35 p.m.

SHRI AUROBINDO

O lord,

Let me

Envisage your desire.

To my soul.

To sworn your vision of annunciation the.

To follow,

My each cell

For transformation

I An great full

To you,

Always,

26-02-2021 morn. 05:30 a.m.

DAY'S OF INCARNATION

All the Specific days like…

Siddhi Diwas.

Darshan day.

Shri Aurobindo Birthday celebration etc.

Are toiling days of premium connected grace's are always present through out HRS.

Provided Receptiveness or gratitude are valid and have deep consensus in heart.

08-03-2021 morn. 60:00 a.m.

SUPERMAN

Gesture of Superman--- Hounding the Universe towards—Real Humanity--- Further Divinity.

It's the Creative part of Dynamic power ---- through Subtle – physic becoming Directive force of evolution.

Where few of Souls are ready for transformation within there magic plan produced by supreme it-self convene Through Great Mother and Shri Aurobindo.

It has been decided since long period of different birth by these two Moderators of Divine Determined faculties from time to time it is mentioned in Letter to Yoga, Evening talks, and Human cycle etc…………..

How ever we people Devotees hence their duties are confirming through their prayers of Instinct knowledge:-

1. How for they have gone.
2. Where they stand.
3. What is their ultimate Aim.

finally who are they at present It's long Journey- to witness thee.

22-03-2021 morn. 06:30 a.m.

LAST COMMANDMENT

By the grace of lord------ and Great Mother:-

You try to emblem last moment of your this birth, you will get amazing HRS since now, then all most every HR, Day, Month, year--- will be collective consciousness to adjudge your destination through whole being ---till soul.

Then your will be alert for any moment when event of joy or trouble you experience try to connect your self with mother to know her almost desire to climb- mountains of your visible object.

Trust faith confidence to the god and know the Hastings.

27-03-2021 morn. 06:30 a.m.

GUIDED MEDITATION

Guided meditation---- it's is energy recycling against Gravitation force going (towards) upward through Superlative position now be more Silence and witness the same.

Pray to mother and have gratification.

Now it's segregation of Desires—one step ahead towards spiritualty confirming Inner consciousness more condensed.

28-03-2021 a.m. 11:00 p.m.

SHRI AUROBINDO

(FOR 5 DECEMBER 1950)

Shri Aurobindo:-

Scale of silence adjudging the smile of Shri Krishna to Entrepreneur the Spiritual Journey towards supramental world.

Here "HE" -- enters into deep Subtle physic for further incarnation.

It's work of aforesaid Agreement between Supreme and Him self.

24-04-2021 night 11:25 p.m.

MOTHER'S ARRIVAL TO INDIA

Orifice of the truth is to be accepted what mother says it should occupy your whole being to entrust consciousness at higher level throughout HRS.

If selected soul is you, then your records of the Past Present and future will tally with final destination of regarded mother.

22-05-2021 night. 10:05 p.m.

AIM

What ever we do where ever we live:-

We must know- our ultimate way, and to follow the destination.

As the aspirations inward the situation then become deep and deep and consciousness adhare the peak Mother may respond the devotion circumstance made up, receptivity grow simultaneously inner being grasp the grace of lord then we are on the right track going towards Sun Lit Path.

The whole being impelling the path of Integral yoga.

Then definitely DAWN will come.

According to readiness the things will happen for new Age.

Dream vision of Shri Aurobindo may come true sole will drive finally after certain pd............. Towards supramental consciousness.

pray and pray prayers must go on........ till the object received.

29-06-2021 morn. 04:00 p.m.

SURRENDER

Over whelming the truth- it is hard to surrender to the mother.

Every hour and very day is - very determined.

your contemplation of desire with mind and heart us gradually deepen, if you are ready on the way of Integral yoga.

SHE – perceives you since beginning step by step.

Who you are to opt this path unless your soul is awaken and offer your self for this mission.

Why you have come here, you must know your object – make your efforts by meditation as you adjudge your- self – as Shri Maa, Shri Aurobindo inspire, you must feel in your inner being.

02-08-2021 morn 05:15 a.m.

SADHNA

They are amused and required one birth more---

Those who have been connected with personal interest and believe system – to different Immortal, Mortal, heads of so called Spiritual sects.

They utilize their mind, wisdom, and vital – to concentrate different life sketches investing most of the period of their life to know, understand by virtue of their Regard.

Some times --- some confusion, conflict carry them to the most of anxiety depressions due to innocent provision of cultivation of Breathings up's and down. you can see the graph gradually lowering their consciousness

It's is not time to divert your central –mood to different deities or Sadguru to find out their grace but to find out your ultimate destination to **"One"** with your whole being.

"Peace" is only one to bring out you form all the unnecessary findings by which you have lost most of the period of your Age.

Determined for the peace—and separate you from different races, by virtue of Instinct.

Your Deep Aspiration is required to search your –self and get update your consciousness because is no time of departure fixed but to know your object finally.

09-08-2021 morn 06:50 a.m.

YOUR MOMENTS

If you connect your last moments with the preserve of present every moment is present HERE then your past and future will be accelerated by Leaps and bounce towards enhance of spiritual condensed consciousness.

So think of present by the total eye of Mother who empire you.

It's very amazing that your living moment are extended from backward to forward (on return basis) lest living moments to adjudge your breathing before going to lap of Mother, that how your births become Loyal to the earnest desire of great supramental truth perceiving your accountability and responsibility towards **Sun Lit Path.**

28-08-2021 morn 05:00 a.m.

DAWN

Preserve this Dawn who inspires you for awaken.

Whole night is full of culmination, and morning is full of pacific consciousness and confidence.

Choice is your's while Sun is at the threshold Reveal the 'condensed' dreams for higher, Mountains by making foundation at the lowest past of your vison -- to be affirmation at the ground level. See the greater Ideas brighter present with the eyes of Instinct hence inner values may be considered for Higher-self and destination of your's ways towards Lights and freedom.

12-09-2021 morn 11:00 a.m

THE MOTHER

→ Only MOTHER can twist your every moment event --- incident --- of your life.

This is "Trust"—ever working since long time, that day and nights may be controlled under her command.

Then <u>Present</u> may be better so Past Future.

26-09-2021 morn. 07:45 a.m.

SADHNA

If you have come to this Earth.....

It is not by chance. It you leave this Earth It is not by chance.

it you think it is opportunity given by God-head then whole meaning is changed.

Hence work hard is only Solution and it should continue till last Breadth........

16-10-2021 morn. 11:15 a.m.

MEETINGS AT A GLANCE

Gesture of collective meetings--- evoke genericization of individual Sadhna,

When Mother's deep convocation for Integral- Yoga ---reaches to the destination of dream vision of Shri Aurobindo, what ever may be future projects by any institution or small centers.

They all are conventions at universal level at Soul consciousness emerging into world- consciousness Pleading by (Spiritual) Bhagwat-Muhurt -hence after one time – one Soul what ever He prays, is all ways inspired by Mother—for Heavenly <u>Supramental -ERA</u> only.

05-12-2021 morn 06:00 a.m.

MAHA SAMADHI DAY

Today is the Day of incorporeal Dedication. With whole being.

Authentic and sustainable Sadhna is required for the purpose of full fill meant of destination – towards divinity and accountability: at the level of Higher consciousness viable to Shri Maa and Shri Aurobindo in true sense.

07-12-2021 morn 08:25 a.m.

TIME

It you Attend the Time—for different spiritual Activities which is real Revelation of God.

After certain pd:

It will go to the deep attention of meditation where every application of thought, request is converted in to dedication if you opt the way of determination of desire is submitted to Supremes desire.

Once, the thing happen with **one-ness** and Time will follow the way of sadhna where you are exact living in spiritual containment pd.

Hence all the circumstances will interlude the passion and sustainability of enthusiasm by mantel, physical then Soul adherence.

16-12-2021 morn 04:15 a.m.

ARDENT FAITH

Your Ardent faith is the complete solution of your problem or Question based on empathetic govern science.

Your destiny has justification for your award for which Nature had already accord sanction for your Action plan.

You are only mid may of the journey of your Spiritual life and surrender tactics.

Whole system is the purpose of your birth and Aim fixed for Sun Lit Path.

The whole energy is invest for the Supreme supplement Desire, where it is seen that how you inspire for One-ness and Sadhna is being done accordingly.

Instinct is the distinction of your ability capability and intuition, Hence your Inner outer consciousness consume for ultimate -- Aim.

When only God is your's and Mother emblem her Blessing and Grace.

Then only you are for the purpose and sake of Supreme in this Universe.

21-12-2021 morn 11:40 a.m.

SHRI AUROBINDO

A FACE OF MAGNIFICATION

It was legend departure to come back again to the new Ere.

It was excellent journey of Shri Aurobindo with commemorative Action --Plan of Supreme assigned by Shri Yogeshwar Krishna.

Let this opportunity become Golden Heaven of Earth.

22-12-2021 morn 11:30 p.m.

SADHNA

You have to review:

Vision of last moment just now: -

To ascertain salvation in all respect and connectivity with your greater -self and Supreme's Desire for purpose of this Birth and progression required for rebirth.

Conscious and subconscious mind and body must adhere with Soul of superb Destination of Spiritual life.

Pray for it.

"Soul" is confirming cementing relationship with the God and your Inner-Self.

01-01-2022 morn 06:00 a.m.

SADHNA

When all the uninvited attractions of wisdom, Mind, Livelihood comfort Zoon – are saturated and Instinet awaken.

Inner consciousness awaken:

Life will get one destination one way to opt only one inspired Gure then rest all will be unutilized.

Then life will be very precious to serve self whole being and others may be persons society relatives country.

Then this birth will get true stairs for upward upto next birth splendid.

Obviously think seriously gorgeously immense fully Silently, Peacefully.

22-02-2022 morn 04:45 a.m.

SEE THE THINGS AS IT IS

If we inter to the space:

Of Spiritual Identity of inventory science.

Then infrastructure of whole being is changed according to inner conscious developed towards surrender.

It is deep desire who:

Console the clearance of Path for Determination of main true object reconciled by aspiration Inspired by Sadguru or Supreme.

We must know the happening around us and influence takes place. Who consider our hour of working towards thought, believe system, relationship and daily routine Life.

24-02-2022 morn 05:45 a.m.

MOTHER

Hospitality of Truth:

For your need it's very Hard to understand.

What mother desires and needs is to verify for your development of Spiritual consciousness is more important.

So every word of Mother may inspire you if you allow your mind, wisdom, and Instinct with total silence.

07-04-2022 morn 6:55 a.m.

SADHNA

All the surgent comprehensive opportunity for Sadhna has been. Provided to you- any where in universe by amalgamating, descending Greater—consciousness beside Sadhna here at Puducherry.

So as to reach affirmative target of Shri Aurobindo........... but connectivity and receptivity must.

07-04-2022 morn 10:30 p.m.

IMPORTANT PD. DATES AT PUDUCHERRY

All the periods important dates at Puducherry and periphery such as Shri Aurobindo arrival at Puducherry and Mother reaches at Puducherry meet with Shri Aurobindo ascending descending Supramental consciousness

May Infront because Present, Past Future, works together as and when required by Spiritual contemplation at forth Dimension.

Clairvoyance adjectives—Supersedes all the Time factors reaches to the Goal of Supreme. Then over mined, Super mined, emblem the Divine project of Heaven.

24-04-2022 morn 07:30 a.m.

THE MOTHER

(102 YEARS OF EXCELLENCE)

Mother finally reached India Puducherry on 24 April 1920.

This annal Day is present always:

Let us see and perceive by Instinet the main object of Shri Maa—Synthesizing Universe, towards Divine purpose object of Supreme ever seen by Shri Aurobindo aggregate the Whole being by meditation gratitude to Shri Maa and Shri Aurobindo with receptive Soul consciousness.

www.ingramcontent.com/pod-product-compliance
Lightning Source LLC
LaVergne TN
LVHW010106170826
845678LV00012B/2270

* 9 7 8 9 3 9 5 7 7 3 6 2 1 *